Bible Walk

A Journey Through Christian Living
and Bible Study

Hartley Edorodion

A Note for the Reader

Welcome! This book is designed so that each chapter stands on its own. Feel free to start reading from any chapter that catches your interest—there's no set order, and you can jump in wherever you like.

In addition, this book can be a versatile resource. It's perfect not just for individual personal devotion, but also for cell groups, home fellowships, Sunday school classes, or any small group gatherings. I hope it enriches your journey in whichever setting you choose to use it.

For more insights, I also share related video teachings on the "Bible Walk" YouTube channel. There, I upload a video for each chapter in a bite-sized format, usually two or three times a week. I invite you to join us there—and while you are there, please don't forget to subscribe, like, share, comment, and click the notification bell for new videos:

https://www.youtube.com/@BibleWalk2.

Some of the chapter titles in this book may appear more than once or seem closely related. This is because several of these messages have been preached and taught at different times, in different settings, and under different inspirations of the Holy Spirit. Each version carries its own emphasis and revelation, even when the topic is similar. I have chosen to include them all so that readers can receive the full depth and richness of the Word as it was given.

I also encourage you to read my other book, Faith That Endures: Trusting God in Every Season. It complements Bible Walk by reminding us that faith is not built in comfort but in consistency—through every season of life. Together, both books are meant to strengthen your relationship with God, deepen your understanding of His Word, and help you walk daily in the light of His promises.

I encourage you to get Bible Walk because I truly believe it should be a companion for every Christian. It is a collection of some of the popular messages I have preached for more than ten years—each chapter reflecting the grace and revelation that God has given me through years of ministry. My prayer is that every page will draw you closer to Jesus, strengthen your faith, deepen your knowledge of His Word, and help you grow in spiritual maturity as you walk daily with Him.

God bless you richly!

— Pastor Hartley Edorodion

Acknowledgement

First and foremost, I give all glory, honour, and praise to the Almighty God — the Author of life, the Fountain of wisdom, and the Inspiration behind every page of this book. Without His guidance, grace, and revelation, *Bible Walk* would have remained only a thought in my heart. To the Holy Spirit, my ever-present Teacher and Companion, thank You for the light and understanding You continue to pour into me daily.

My deepest appreciation goes to our Lord and Saviour Jesus Christ, whose Word is the very essence of this work. Every truth written here flows from His Word — the living Word that brings light to every dark path and life to every weary soul.

I also express heartfelt gratitude to my family for their love, patience, and unwavering support throughout the preparation of this book. Your encouragement has been a pillar of strength and inspiration.

To the members of *Complete Christianity and Holy Ghost Power Ministry*, thank you for your prayers, partnership, and commitment to the vision of spreading God's Word. You are part of this divine journey, and your faith continues to inspire me.

I am equally grateful to every reader, believer, and student of the Word who seeks to grow deeper in their relationship with God. *Bible Walk* was written for you — that through its pages, you may find illumination, transformation, and renewed strength in your spiritual walk.

Finally, to all who contributed in one way or another — through counsel, prayer, or encouragement — may the Lord reward your labour of love abundantly.

To God alone be all the glory.

— Pastor Hartley Edorodion
Author, Bible Walk

Copyright

© 2025 Pastor Hartley Edorodion
All rights reserved.

No part of this publication may be reproduced, stored in a retrieval system, or transmitted in any form or by any means — electronic, mechanical, photocopying, recording, or otherwise — without prior written permission from the author or publisher, except in the case of brief quotations used in critical articles or reviews.

Scripture quotations are taken from the King James Version (KJV) of the Holy Bible, which is in the public domain, except where otherwise stated.

ISBN: 978-1-9192829-0-9
First Edition, 2025

All rights of the author have been asserted.

For information, permissions, or ministry resources, please contact:

Email: edorodion@hotmail.com

"Thy word is a lamp unto my feet, and a light unto my path." — Psalm 119:105

Preface

The Bible Walk was born out of a deep desire to help believers not only read the Scriptures but truly walk through them — chapter by chapter, lesson by lesson. It is a journey through the Word of God, designed to open hearts, strengthen faith, and bring practical understanding to the timeless truths of Scripture.

For many Christians, the Bible can sometimes feel like a vast landscape — rich, yet overwhelming; ancient, yet alive. Bible Walk seeks to make that landscape familiar, helping every reader experience the Word not as a distant history book, but as a living guide to everyday life. Each chapter explores foundational truths that shape our relationship with God, ourselves, and others.

This work is written with simplicity and clarity so that everyone — from new believers to seasoned Christians — can understand, reflect, and apply the teachings. It invites the reader to walk slowly, thoughtfully, and prayerfully through Scripture, discovering along the way the power of faith, love, humility, obedience, service, and spiritual growth.

The Bible Walk is not just a book to be read but a journey to be lived. It challenges the mind, stirs the heart, and transforms the spirit. Each chapter ends with interactive Q&A (interactive questions and answers) and reflection points to help readers think deeply and apply what they have learned to their daily walk with God.

My prayer is that as you go through these pages, the Holy Spirit will speak to you personally. May your understanding of God's Word deepen, your faith be strengthened, and your Christian journey become more fruitful and fulfilling.

May every step you take through this Bible Walk draw you closer to the One who said, "I am the way, the truth, and the life." (John 14:6)

— Pastor Hartley Edorodion

Senior Pastor, Complete Christianity & Holy Ghost Power Ministry

Contents

A Note for the Reader ……………...………..…..…… ……..i

Acknowledgement …………………………………..… …...ii

Copyright …… ……………………………………....…..iv

Preface ……………………………………………..…....v

Introduction ………………………………………....…xi

Chapter 1 Love and Unity 1

Chapter 2 Living Free from Condemnation: Walking in the Spirit..8

Chapter 3 The Blessing of the Lord 15

Chapter 4 Idolatry – The Rival of True Worship...............22

Chapter 5 The Sheep and the Goats 29

Chapter 6 The Armour of God – Standing Strong in Spiritual Warfare 36

Chapter 7 The Great Commission and Soul Winning.........44

Chapter 8 Giving in the New Testament 51

Chapter 9 Greed: The Silent Enemy of the Soul.................58

Chapter 10 Be Not Drunk with Wine, But Filled with the Spirit...65

Chapter 11 Pride: The Hidden Destroyer...........................72

Chapter 12 Faith in Action – Closing the Gap Between Knowing and Doing..78

Chapter 13 Fear Not – Living in Courage and Faith...........85

Chapter 14 Character and Integrity – The True Image 93

Chapter 15 The Sabbath – Christ Our True Rest...............100

Chapter 16 Fear – The Silent Thief of Faith 106

Chapter 17 From Gift to Skill – Excelling in Your God-Given Calling 113

Chapter 18 Power – The Evidence of the Kingdom 120

Chapter 19 Fasting – The Hidden Strength of the Believer 126

(Matthew 6:16–18)..126

Chapter 20 Prayer – The Strongest Weapon of the Believer 133

Chapter 21 Healing – The Children's Bread 140

Chapter 22 Water Baptism – Buried with Christ, Raised to New Life...146

Chapter 23 Baptism of the Holy Spirit – Endued with Power from on High..155

Chapter 24 Easter – The Power of the Resurrection 163

Chapter 25 Training Up a Child in the Way of the Lord..169

Chapter 26 Grace, Not Competition..................................175

Chapter 27 Christ's Second Coming – The Last Prophecy 181

Chapter 28 End Time Signs and Precautions 188

Chapter 29 The Joy of the Lord: Your Strength 194

Chapter 30 Love – The Greatest Commandment.............201

Chapter 31 Prayer – The Lifeline of the Christian 207

Chapter 32 Make Hay While the Sun Shines – Avoiding Delay and Procrastination 214

Chapter 33 Taming the Tongue: A Test of True Faith 220

Chapter 34 Knowledge and Wisdom 226

Chapter 35 Knowledge, Understanding, and Wisdom 232

Chapter 36 Sowing and Reaping 239

Chapter 37 Unforgiveness – The Enemy of Progress 245

Chapter 38 The Rebellious Child and the Compassionate Father: Sin, Repentance, and Restoration 251

Chapter 39 Jesus: The Way, The Truth, and The Life 257

Chapter 40 Anger – Enemy at the Edge of Breakthrough. 266

Chapter 41 Self-Esteem — Knowing Your Worth in Christ 272

Chapter 42 The Authenticity and Infallibility of God's Word 278

Chapter 43 Time Management 284

Chapter 44 Thinking Positively Out of the Box 290

Chapter 45 Breaking the Spirit of Poverty 296

Chapter 46 Relationship at Home 302

Chapter 47 Proof of Honour – Honouring God with Your Substance 310

Chapter 48 The Power of Praises 317

Chapter 49 The Power and Purpose of Worship 322

Chapter 50 The Power of Praise and Worship Combined .328

Chapter 51 The Reality of the Spiritual World.................334

Chapter 52 He Will Do It 341

Chapter 53 Christmas — Celebrating Christ, Not Just a Day 348

Chapter 54 Holy Communion — Remembering the Covenant 355

Chapter 55 The Rapture: The Blessed Hope of Believers 361

Chapter 56 Holiness — The Beauty of God's Nature 368

Chapter 57 Do Not Be Anxious About Anything.............376

Chapter 58 Idea, Goal, Planning, and Action....................383

Chapter 59 Breaking Free from Financial Debt................389

Chapter 60 Marriage: As Ordained by God 396

Chapter 61 Spiritual Growth and Maturity 404

Chapter 62 The Gifts of the Spirit......................................410

About the Author...417

Introduction

The Bible is not just a book — it is the living Word of God. Every page breathes His wisdom, every story reveals His heart, and every commandment leads us toward a life of purpose, victory, and eternal hope. Yet, for many believers, the Bible remains an unopened treasure, a vast landscape left unexplored.

Bible Walk was written to change that. It is an invitation to walk through Scripture one chapter at a time — to see, hear, and understand God in a deeper and more personal way. Each chapter is not simply a teaching, but a journey. It opens with the Word, explains the truth within, and guides readers toward application in daily living. The aim is not just to fill the mind with knowledge, but to transform the heart and renew the spirit.

This walk through the Bible covers vital themes for every believer: love, unity, humility, prayer, forgiveness, faith, service, wisdom, the second coming of Christ, and so much more. These are not random topics but stepping stones on a path of spiritual growth. Each lesson is anchored in Scripture, written in practical language, and designed to awaken both new believers and mature Christians to a more vibrant walk with God.

Life itself is a journey — one filled with decisions, challenges, and seasons. Bible Walk reminds us that in every season, God speaks. Through His Word, He comforts, corrects, strengthens, and directs us. Like a lamp to our feet and a light to our path (Psalm 119:105), the Bible illuminates the way we must go, even when the road is uncertain.

This book also serves as a teaching and reflection tool. At the end of each chapter, you will find reflection questions meant to stir thought, inspire conversation, and lead to prayer. These are not meant to be academic tests but spiritual mirrors — to help you see how the Word connects to your personal life, relationships, and calling.

Above all, Bible Walk is a reminder that walking with God requires consistency. It is not a sprint but a lifelong journey. Every day, every step, and every choice draws us closer or farther from Him. My prayer is that as you read these pages, your heart will be stirred again to love God more deeply, to follow Christ more faithfully, and to live by the power of the Holy Spirit more boldly.

Let each chapter become a moment of encounter — a time to pause, reflect, and realign with the voice of God. May the Word not only be studied but lived. For it is not enough to hear; true blessing comes when we obey.

Welcome to Bible Walk — your step-by-step journey through the living Word. May each lesson light your path and lead you closer to the heart of God.

Chapter 1

Love and Unity
(Psalm 133)

> *"Behold, how good and how pleasant it is for brethren to dwell together in unity!" (Psalm 133:1)*

Introduction

Unity is one of the most beautiful gifts God has given His people, yet it is also one of the most fragile. From families to churches, division has always been a threat. Psalm 133 celebrates the blessing of believers dwelling together in harmony, describing it as both "good and pleasant." Unity not only brings peace among men, but also attracts the commanded blessing of God. In a divided world, Christians are called to display the power of love and unity as a living witness of Christ.

The Beauty of Unity

Unity is not just a good idea — it is God's design. David describes it as both good and pleasant because it brings peace and joy to everyone involved.

The reverse is also true: "Behold, how bad and unpleasant it is for brethren to dwell together in disunity!" Where there is strife, quarrelling, and hatred, no one thrives.

Unity flows from love. Disunity flows from the absence of love. (1 John 4:18). True love eliminates distance, while hatred creates barriers. Love is not an option for Christians — it is a command (John 13:34–35; Matthew 22:37–40), a mark of discipleship (1 John 3:10–18), and the very nature of God Himself (1 John 4:7–8, 20–21).

Unity in the Early Church

The early church experienced explosive growth because of their love and unity:

"The multitude of them that believed were of one heart and of one soul ... and great grace was upon them all" (Acts 4:32–33).

Unity produced shared vision, mutual care, spiritual power, and abundant grace. Even the human body teaches us this lesson: every organ must work in harmony for life to flourish. The tongue and the teeth may clash, but they reconcile immediately. So must believers.

The Necessity of Unity

Jesus Himself declared: "If a kingdom be divided against itself, that kingdom cannot stand. And if a house be divided against itself, that house cannot stand" (Mark 3:24–25).

This principle applies to nations, families, churches, ministries, and even businesses. Anything divided will eventually collapse. Unity is not optional — it is essential.

Different Ways Unity Can Be Achieved

Human societies achieve unity in different ways. Some are temporary, others genuine:

1. Love – the most authentic and lasting form of unity. This is the Christian way.

2. Covenant – unity enforced through oaths or pledges (e.g., gangs or cults).
3. Promises and Vows – often seen in marriage and friendships.
4. Laws and Rules – governments, organizations, and companies rely on this.

But for Christians, the only enduring unity is unity born of love (Philippians 2:2; Ephesians 4:1–3).

Unity is a Choice

God will not force unity on anyone. Each believer must choose whether to love or to hate, to reconcile or to divide.

- "Let brotherly love continue" (Hebrews 13:1).
- "Consider one another to provoke unto love and good works" (Hebrews 10:24).
- "Follow peace with all men, and holiness, without which no man shall see the Lord" (Hebrews 12:14).

When we choose unity, God commands His blessing (Psalm 133:3).

The Danger of Isolation

Some Christians today refuse to belong to a local church, claiming "Christianity is in the heart." They become lone rangers, sometimes joining online services but avoiding physical gatherings.

The Bible warns against this: "Not forsaking the assembling of ourselves together, as the manner of some is …" (Hebrews 10:25).

Online fellowship can help in certain seasons, but it cannot replace real fellowship. A local church knows you personally, prays with you, supports you in times of need, and holds you accountable.

Practical Steps Toward Unity

- Forgive quickly — don't let grudges grow.
- Speak truth in love — resolve conflicts honestly but gently.
- Refuse gossip — silence strife before it spreads.
- Support your church — commit your time, gifts, and resources.
- Pray for unity — ask God to bind hearts together in His love.

Interactive Q&A

Q1: Why is unity important in the church?
A1: Without unity, the church cannot stand or fulfil its mission (Mark 3:25; Acts 4:32–33).

Q2: Can unity exist without love?
A2: Yes, but it will be temporary. Only love produces lasting unity (John 13:34–35).

Q3: What blessings come from unity?
A3: God commands blessing, grace increases, power is released, and the world sees Christ (Psalm 133:3; Acts 2:1–4).

Q4: Why can't online fellowship replace local church gatherings?
A4: Because only a local church provides physical presence, care, and accountability (Hebrews 10:25).

Q5: What practical steps can strengthen unity in a congregation?
A5: Forgiveness, humility, encouragement, shared vision, and focusing on Christ (Ephesians 4:1–3).

Reflection Points

- Do I bring unity or division where I am?
- Have I been tempted to isolate myself instead of engaging in

fellowship?
- What step can I take this week to strengthen unity in my church or family?

Closing Prayer

Lord, thank You for the gift of love and unity in the body of Christ. Forgive me for times I contributed to strife or isolation. Fill me with Your Spirit so that I may walk in humility, forgiveness, and love. Unite our churches, families, and communities so that the world may see Jesus in us. In His name we pray, Amen.

Chapter 2

Living Free from Condemnation: Walking in the Spirit

(Romans 8:1; John 8:1–11)

"There is therefore now no condemnation to them which are in Christ Jesus, who walk not after the flesh, but after the Spirit." (Romans 8:1)

"When Jesus had lifted up himself, and saw none but the woman, he said unto her, Woman, where are those thine accusers? hath no man condemned thee? She said, No man, Lord. And Jesus said unto her, Neither do I condemn thee: go, and sin no more." (John 8:10–11)

Introduction

Condemnation is a prison many believers live in unnecessarily. Some are haunted by their past mistakes, others by the accusations of people, and still others by the voice of the enemy (the devil). But Scripture declares with authority: "Now no condemnation."

Romans 8:1 speaks of a legal verdict — that those in Christ are no longer under guilt or penalty. John 8 shows us how that verdict plays out in real life: a woman guilty of sin stood before Christ, but instead of condemnation she received mercy, forgiveness, and a new beginning.

What Condemnation Really Is

Condemnation is the gavel of guilt — the declaration that you are unworthy, disqualified, or hopeless. It can come from three sources:
- The devil – the accuser of the brethren (Revelation 12:10).
- People – critics, judges, or those who refuse to forget your past.
- Yourself – self-condemnation is often harsher than anything external.

But Jesus demonstrates in John 8 that condemnation is never His heart for the repentant. He did not excuse sin, but He removed condemnation.

Conviction vs. Condemnation

The woman in John 8 was guilty — yet Christ's response shows the difference:
- The Pharisees wanted to condemn her to death.
- Jesus convicted her to repentance and gave her a new beginning.

It is important to distinguish between the conviction of the Holy Spirit and the condemnation of the enemy:

- Conviction comes from the Holy Spirit to lead us to repentance and restoration. It is gentle, kind, and lifts once repentance occurs.
- Condemnation comes from the devil to produce shame, despair, and bondage. It is harsh, persistent, and continues even after repentance.

Key Differences:
- Conviction is for correction; condemnation is for destruction.
- Conviction leads to life and peace; condemnation leads to guilt and death.
- Conviction is temporary until repentance; condemnation is continuous and tormenting.
- Conviction ends in freedom and joy; condemnation traps in bondage and sorrow.

Jesus embodies conviction without condemnation. His words to the woman were both merciful and purposeful: "Neither do I condemn thee... go, and sin no more" (John

8:11). He lifted her from shame and pointed her to transformation.

Why There Is No Condemnation in Christ

1. Christ took our punishment – The woman was spared because Christ Himself would soon bear her sin at the cross (Isaiah 53:5).
2. We are declared new – "If any man be in Christ, he is a new creature: old things are passed away; behold, all things are become new." (2 Corinthians 5:17).
3. God remembers sin no more – "Their sins and iniquities will I remember no more" (Hebrews 10:17).
4. The Spirit affirms liberty – "Where the Spirit of the Lord is, there is liberty" (2 Corinthians 3:17).

If Jesus — the only sinless One — says "Neither do I condemn thee," who else has the right to condemn?

Walking in the Spirit, Not the Flesh

Romans 8:1 ties freedom from condemnation to walking in the Spirit.
- Walking in the flesh: like the Pharisees, living in judgment, hypocrisy, and sin.
- Walking in the Spirit: like the forgiven woman, living in obedience and gratitude to God.

The Spirit-filled life does not excuse sin; it empowers victory over sin. Jesus' words were both release ("Neither do I condemn thee") and responsibility ("Go, and sin no more"). Grace saves us, but the Spirit leads us into holiness.

Breaking Free from Condemnation

1. Accept Christ's Verdict – Believe His word: "No condemnation."
2. Reject Accusations – Silence the Pharisee voices around and within you.
3. Renew Your Mind – Replace lies with God's truth (Romans 12:2).
4. Forgive Yourself – If Christ remembers your sin no more, neither should you.
5. Walk in the Spirit – Live daily with the Spirit's guidance and power.

Interactive Q&A

Q1: What is condemnation, and how is it different from conviction?
A1: Condemnation is the enemy's tool of guilt and destruction. Conviction is the Spirit's gentle prompting to repentance. Jesus condemned no one but convicted many (John 8:10–11).

Q2: Why is there no condemnation for those in Christ?
A2: Because Christ bore our punishment at the cross, made us new creations, and God now remembers our sins no more (Romans 8:1; 2 Corinthians 5:17; Hebrews 10:17).

Q3: What lesson does the story of the adulterous woman teach us?
A3: That Jesus offers mercy instead of condemnation, but also calls us to repentance and holy living — "Neither do I condemn thee… go, and sin no more."

Q4: How can a believer break free from condemnation?
A4: By accepting Christ's verdict of freedom, rejecting accusations, renewing the mind with Scripture, forgiving oneself, and walking in the Spirit.

Q5: What happens when we walk in the Spirit instead of the flesh?
A5: We experience liberty, peace, and life. Walking in the flesh leads to bondage and guilt, but walking in the Spirit leads to joy, victory, and freedom (Romans 8:6).

Reflection Points

- Do I confuse the Spirit's conviction with Satan's condemnation?
- Have I fully embraced Christ's verdict of "no condemnation"?
- Do I still listen to Pharisee voices of accusation in my life?
- How can I walk daily in the Spirit so that I live free from

condemnation?

- In what ways can I extend the same mercy to others that Christ extended to the woman in John 8?

Closing Prayer

Lord Jesus, thank You for declaring over me, "Neither do I condemn thee." Help me to live in the liberty You purchased at the cross. Silence the voices of accusation in my heart and remind me of Your Word. Fill me with Your Spirit so I may walk in holiness, peace, and victory. Teach me to extend the same mercy to others that You have extended to me. In Your mighty name, Amen.

Chapter 3

The Blessing of the Lord
(Proverbs 10:22)

"The blessing of the LORD, it maketh rich, and he addeth no sorrow with it." (Proverbs 10:22)

Introduction

Every human being desires a life of abundance, peace, and success, but the path to lasting prosperity is not found in hard work or worldly systems. True prosperity flows from the blessing of the Lord (Proverbs 10:22). This blessing is the divine empowerment that brings increase without sorrow. Worldly riches often come with fear, anxiety, and compromise, but the blessing of God enriches life in every dimension — spiritually, physically, emotionally, and financially — and adds no sorrow.

What Is the Blessing of the Lord?

The blessing of the Lord is not merely material wealth. It is God's divine favour and empowerment for success. It is the presence of God working actively in your life, guiding your decisions, and prospering the work of your hands. When you walk in the blessing, you carry God's grace into every situation, and everything you touch begins to flourish. This blessing cannot be imitated or replaced by human effort — it is supernatural.

The Difference Between Riches and Blessing

There are many who have riches but no rest. They possess wealth yet lack joy and peace. The riches that come from the world often demand compromise, but the riches that come from God are accompanied by righteousness, peace, and joy. The blessing of the Lord aligns your wealth with His will and fills it with purpose. You do not just become rich — you become fulfilled.

God's Desire for His Children

It has never been God's will for His children to live in poverty, shame, or lack. From the beginning, His covenant included prosperity, health, and peace. 'But thou shalt remember the LORD thy God: for it is he that giveth thee power to get wealth, that he may establish his covenant' (Deuteronomy 8:18). Yet, the purpose of wealth in God's kingdom is not self-glorification — it is service. God blesses us so that we can bless others (Genesis 12:2). True prosperity is not measured by what you have, but by what you give and the lives you impact.

The Source of True Prosperity

The source of true prosperity is God alone. Every good and perfect gift comes from Him (James 1:17). Worldly prosperity may come through manipulation or corruption, but divine prosperity comes through obedience, faith, and righteousness. When the Lord blesses, He not only provides resources but also grants wisdom to manage them and peace to enjoy them. 'Riches and honour are with me; yea, durable riches and righteousness' (Proverbs 8:18).

Why Many Believers Struggle Financially

If God desires that His children prosper, why do many still live in lack? Several reasons include:

1. Lack of Knowledge — Many do not understand God's covenant principles on stewardship, and giving.

2. Limited Capacity — God does not pour abundance into unprepared vessels. Growth in discipline and wisdom increases capacity.

3. Wrong Priorities — Some pursue money rather than the presence of God, forgetting that wealth follows divine purpose.

4. Fear and Doubt — Unbelief limits divine supply. Faith opens doors to supernatural provision.

Walking in the Blessing

To walk in the blessing of the Lord means to live under His direction and in His will. Here are principles for walking in it:

1. Seek First the Kingdom (Matthew 6:33) — Make God's purpose your top priority, and everything else will follow.

2. Walk in Obedience (Deuteronomy 28:1–2) — Blessing is the fruit of obedience.

3. Give Generously (Luke 6:38; 2 Corinthians 9:6–8) — Giving creates room for increase and divine favour.

4. Live with Integrity (Proverbs 11:3) — God cannot bless dishonesty or greed.

5. Stay Grateful and Humble (Deuteronomy 8:11–18) — Gratitude preserves blessings; pride drives them away.

Riches Without Sorrow

When your riches come from the Lord, they will not destroy you. Divine blessing adds peace, not pain; joy, not burden. It does not cause family division, sleeplessness, or guilt. God's blessing prospers both your soul and your substance. When you live under His favour, wealth becomes a tool, not a trap. It becomes a channel for generosity and worship.

The Blessing of the Lord is All-inclusive

The blessing of the Lord is more than possessions — it is all-inclusive. It is complete, it transforms every aspect of your life. It is the presence of God that is the blessing. So, it is important to seek the Blesser, not merely the blessing. When God is your portion, everything you need follows naturally (Matthew 6:33). Let your goal be to live in His will, walk in His peace, and bless others through what He gives you.

Interactive Q&A

Q1: What is the blessing of the Lord?
A1: It is God's divine empowerment that brings true wealth, peace, and joy without sorrow.

Q2: Can God make someone rich?
A2: Yes. God gives power to get wealth to establish His covenant (Deuteronomy 8:18).

Q3: Does poverty guarantee heaven?
A3: No. Salvation through Christ, not poverty, determines eternal life.

Q4: Are there other sources of blessing?
A4: Yes, but worldly blessings bring sorrow, fear, and destruction.

Q5: What should a believer's focus be?
A5: Seeking first the kingdom of God and His righteousness (Matthew 6:33).

Reflection Points

- Do I pursue the blessing or the Blesser?
- Am I using my resources to glorify God and serve others?
- Do I trust God as the source of all my provision?
- How can I cultivate gratitude and generosity in my

prosperity?
- Am I walking in obedience that invites divine blessing?

Closing Prayer

Father, thank You for being the source of every true blessing. Teach me to seek You above all things. Deliver me from greed and fear, and help me walk in integrity and faith. May Your blessing rest upon my life — wealth without sorrow, peace without anxiety, and joy without end. Use me to bless others as You have blessed me. In Jesus' name, Amen.

Chapter 4

Idolatry – The Rival of True Worship

(Exodus 20:3–5)

"Thou shalt have no other gods before me. Thou shalt not make unto thee any graven image ... Thou shalt not bow down thyself to them, nor serve them: for I the LORD thy God am a jealous God." (Exodus 20:3–5)

Introduction

Idolatry is as old as humanity's rebellion and as current as today's culture. While most people imagine idols as carved statues or golden calves, idolatry goes far deeper. An idol is anything that takes the place of God in our hearts, our trust, or our devotion.

From Genesis to Revelation, the Bible consistently warns against idolatry. God alone is worthy of worship, and He calls His people to love Him with all their heart, soul, mind, and strength (Deuteronomy 6:5; Mark 12:30).

The Seriousness of Idolatry

Idolatry is not just one sin among many; it is the root sin that leads to countless others. When people worship anything other than God, they open the door to immorality, injustice, oppression, and destruction. Paul explained that when humanity turned from God, they exchanged His glory for images and fell into every kind of wickedness (Romans 1:21–23). Thus, idolatry is the fountainhead of rebellion against God.

Idolatry as Spiritual Adultery

Throughout Scripture, God portrays His covenant with His people as a marriage. When Israel turned to idols, the prophets described it as adultery. Hosea's life was a living parable of God's grief over His people's unfaithfulness (Hosea 1–3). Idolatry is not simply breaking a command; it is breaking God's heart. It is giving the love and devotion due to the Creator to something created.

Idolatry in Israel's History

The history of Israel illustrates the dangers of idolatry:
- The Golden Calf: When Moses delayed on Mount Sinai, the people demanded idols. They worshipped a golden calf, breaking the first three commandments at once (Exodus 32:1–6).
- The Kings of Israel: Solomon, though wise, fell into idolatry through foreign wives (1 Kings 11:4). Other kings built high places and altars to Baal, leading to national judgment.
- The Prophets' Warnings: Isaiah, Jeremiah, and Ezekiel repeatedly rebuked the people for forsaking the living God for powerless idols.

Idolatry always leads to judgment because it is spiritual adultery against God.

The New Testament on Idolatry

Idolatry did not vanish with the Old Testament. The New Testament continues to warn against it:

- Paul wrote: "Flee from idolatry" (1 Corinthians 10:14).
- John warned: "Little children, keep yourselves from idols"

(1 John 5:21).
- Colossians 3:5 equates covetousness with idolatry.

In the New Testament, idolatry is not just about statues but about misplaced loves, loyalties, and desires.

Modern Forms of Idolatry

Today, idols may not be golden calves, but they are everywhere:

- Money and materialism – trusting wealth instead of God (Matthew 6:24).
- Pleasure and entertainment – prioritizing comfort over holiness.
- Relationships – placing people above God's will.
- Self – living for ego, pride, or self-image.
- Job and career – when work consumes all attention and time, leaving little room for God.
- Hobbies and interests – when leisure activities or personal passions take priority over devotion to Christ.
- Technology and culture – giving devotion to things that distract from God.

Often, idols are not evil in themselves. They may be good gifts of God, but when they take first place in our hearts, they become destructive. Idolatry is when good things become ultimate things.

The Futility of Idols

The prophets mocked the foolishness of idols: "They have mouths, but they speak not: eyes have they, but they see not ... They that make them are like unto them" (Psalm 115:5–8). Idols are powerless to save, but powerful to enslave. They cannot hear our cries or deliver our souls. Those who worship them become spiritually blind and deaf, hardened in sin.

God's Call to Exclusive Worship

God is a jealous God — not in a sinful way, but in His holy desire for His people's undivided love. Idolatry robs God of glory and robs us of true life.

Jesus reaffirmed the greatest commandment: "Thou shalt worship the Lord thy God, and him only shalt thou serve" (Matthew 4:10). Only God deserves first place.

True freedom is found not in serving idols but in worshiping God through Christ in Spirit and in truth (John 4:23–24).

Victory Over Idolatry

Jesus showed us how to overcome idolatry. When tempted by Satan to bow down for worldly gain, He answered: "Thou shalt worship the Lord thy God, and him only shalt thou serve" (Matthew 4:10). At the cross, He disarmed principalities and powers (Colossians 2:15), breaking the chains of sin and idolatry.

Believers overcome idolatry by fixing their hearts on Christ, being filled with the Holy Spirit, and walking in obedience to God's Word. Worship is the weapon that defeats idolatry — when God is enthroned in our hearts, all other idols lose their grip.

Interactive Q&A

Q1: What is idolatry?
A1: Idolatry is worshiping, trusting, or loving anything more than God — whether physical images, material possessions, desires, or self.

Q2: How did idolatry affect Israel in the Old Testament?
A2: It led to national sin and judgment. From the golden calf to the kings who worshipped Baal, idolatry brought shame and destruction (Exodus 32; 1 Kings 11).

Q3: What does the New Testament say about idolatry?
A3: It warns believers to flee from idolatry (1 Corinthians 10:14) and teaches that even covetousness and misplaced desires are forms of idolatry (Colossians 3:5).

Q4: What are some modern idols?
A4: Money, pleasure, relationships, self, job, hobbies, fame,

and technology. Anything that takes God's place in our hearts can become an idol.

Q5: How can a Christian overcome idolatry?
A5: By putting God first, surrendering every area of life to Him, staying rooted in His Word, worshiping Him in Spirit and truth, and being filled with the Holy Spirit (Matthew 4:10; John 4:23–24).

Reflection Points

- Are there hidden idols in my heart that compete with God?
- Do I trust wealth, people, or myself more than I trust God?
- Have I made job, hobbies, or entertainment into priorities over obedience?
- Do I truly worship God with undivided devotion?
- What practical steps can I take to tear down idols and give God first place?

Closing Prayer

Heavenly Father, I confess that many times I have allowed other things to take Your place in my heart. Forgive me for idols of self, money, pleasure, pride, job, or hobbies. Today I surrender all to You. Be Lord of my life in every area. Teach me to worship You in Spirit and truth, and deliver me from every hidden idol. Let my heart be wholly Yours. In Jesus' name, Amen.

Chapter 5

The Sheep and the Goats
(Matthew 25:31–46)

"When the Son of man shall come in his glory, and all the holy angels with him, then shall he sit upon the throne of his glory: And before him shall be gathered all nations: and he shall separate them one from another, as a shepherd divideth his sheep from the goats: And he shall set the sheep on his right hand, but the goats on the left." (Matthew 25:31–33)

Introduction

One of the most sobering passages in the teachings of Jesus is His description of the final judgment, where He separates the sheep from the goats. This parable reminds us that Christianity is not only about what we believe or pray, but also about how we live. Acts of love, compassion, and service are not optional extras; they are evidence of true faith. This chapter challenges us to examine whether we are living as sheep who serve Christ by serving others, or as goats who neglect the very things God values most.

Context of Matthew 25

Matthew 25 presents three related parables:
1. The Ten Virgins (vv. 1–13) – Watchfulness: Christians must be spiritually alert and ready.
2. The Talents (vv. 14–30) – Faithfulness: Christians must use their resources for God's Kingdom.
3. The Sheep and the Goats (vv. 31–46) – Righteousness in Action: Christians must live out love in practical ways.

All three emphasize readiness for Christ's return, but readiness is proven not just by waiting, but by working and walking in love.

Who Are the Sheep and the Goats?

This passage is often misunderstood as dividing believers from unbelievers. But notice:
- Both groups call Jesus "Lord" (vv. 37, 44).

- Only those led by the Spirit can sincerely do this (1 Corinthians 12:3).

Therefore, this is about two kinds of Christians:
- The Sheep: faithful, obedient, compassionate.
- The Goats: careless, self-centered, negligent.

"All nations" in this context refers to Christians from every tribe, denomination, and background.

The Sin of Commission and the Sin of Omission

The goats were not condemned for what they did wrong, but for what they failed to do.

- Sins of Commission – committing what is forbidden: adultery, lying, idolatry, hatred, and so on (Galatians 5:19–21).
- Sins of Omission – failing to do what is right: refusing to love, help, care, or give (James 4:17).

The goats' sin was omission. They did not feed the hungry, clothe the naked, or visit the sick. Many Christians avoid sins of commission but fall into omission daily.

Doing Good to Others equals Doing It to Christ

The goats failed because they thought serving Christ meant only serving Him directly. They missed the deeper truth:
- "Inasmuch as ye have done it unto one of the least of these my brethren, ye have done it unto me." (v. 40)
- "Inasmuch as ye did it not ... ye did it not to me." (v. 45)

To serve others is to serve Christ. To ignore others is to ignore Christ.

Judgment and Reward

The sheep and goats face very different outcomes:
- To the sheep: "Come, ye blessed of my Father, inherit the kingdom prepared for you ..." (v. 34).
- To the goats: "Depart from me, ye cursed, into everlasting fire ..." (v. 41).
- Final verdict: "The righteous into life eternal, but the wicked into everlasting punishment" (v. 46).

Faith without works is dead (James 2:14–18). Our works do not save us, but they prove the reality of our faith.

Prayer Is Not Enough

Prayer is vital, but prayer alone is not sufficient. James makes it plain:

"If a brother or sister be naked, and destitute of daily food, And one of you say unto them, Depart in peace, be ye warmed and filled; notwithstanding ye give them not those things which are needful to the body; what doth it profit? Even so faith, if it hath not works, is dead." (James 2:15–17)

True Christianity is not just what we pray, but what we do.

Lessons for Today's Church

- Many believers today are goats not because they do evil, but because they refuse to do good.
- Some excuse themselves with words like: "I'll pray for you" — when God wants them to act.
- Practical love — food, clothing, encouragement, time, presence — is as spiritual as prayer.
- True sheep live in compassion, generosity, and service.

Interactive Q&A

Q1: Who are the sheep and goats in this passage?
A1: They represent two groups of Christians — those who

obey Christ by doing good (sheep), and those who neglect to do good (goats).

Q2: What are the two types of sin in Christianity?
A2: Sins of commission (committing evil) and sins of omission (failing to do good).

Q3: Why were the goats condemned?
A3: Not for evil acts, but for neglecting acts of love and service (Matthew 25:42–45).

Q4: What reward do the sheep receive?
A4: Eternal life and inheritance of God's Kingdom (Matthew 25:34, 46).

Q5: Is prayer enough when someone is in need?
A5: No. Prayer must be joined with action. Faith without works is dead (James 2:14–18).

Reflection Points

- Am I guilty of omission — failing to do good when I could?
- Do I recognize that serving people is serving Christ Himself?
- Do I tend to offer words ("I'll pray for you") when God is calling me to act?
- Am I living as a sheep or as a goat?

Closing Prayer

Lord Jesus, thank You for showing us that true faith works through love. Forgive me for times I have failed to do good. Open my eyes to see You in the needs of others, and help me to act with compassion. May I live as one of Your sheep, ready to inherit the Kingdom. In Your name I pray, Amen.

Chapter 6

The Armour of God – Standing Strong in Spiritual Warfare

(Ephesians 6:10–18)

"Finally, my brethren, be strong in the Lord, and in the power of his might. Put on the whole armour of God, that ye may be able to stand against the wiles of the devil. For we wrestle not against flesh and blood, but against principalities, against powers, against the rulers of the darkness of this world, against spiritual wickedness in high places. Wherefore take unto you the whole armour of God, that ye may be able to withstand in the evil day, and having done all, to stand." (Ephesians 6:10–13)

Introduction

Every believer is in a battle, whether they recognize it or not. Paul makes it clear that our struggle is not against flesh and blood but against unseen spiritual forces. To stand strong, Christians must be fully equipped with the armour of God. Spiritual warfare is not a distant concept; it is part of daily life when we face temptation, discouragement, and opposition. This chapter shows how each piece of God's armour equips us to live in victory, not defeat, and to stand firm against the schemes of the enemy.

1. The Reality of Spiritual Warfare

1.1 The Enemy's Schemes

Paul warns us to stand against "the wiles of the devil" (v. 11). The devil's tactics include deception (Genesis 3:1–5), division (Mark 3:25), discouragement (1 Kings 19:4), and distraction (Luke 10:40). He rarely attacks openly; he prefers to trick us into blaming people instead of recognizing him as the real enemy.

1.2 The Invisible War

"We wrestle not against flesh and blood" (v. 12). Our real battle is not with family, neighbours, or colleagues, but with unseen spiritual forces: principalities, powers, rulers of darkness, and spiritual wickedness. This is why human strength, intelligence, or resources are insufficient. The war is spiritual; we need spiritual weapons.

1.3 The Evil Day

Paul says, "that ye may be able to withstand in the evil day" (v. 13). Every believer will face seasons of testing. "Evil days" can include temptation, persecution, crisis, sickness, doubt, or loss. In such moments, only those anchored in God's strength will stand.

2. The Call to Strength

2.1 Not Our Strength, But His

Paul does not say, "Be strong in yourself." He says, "Be strong in the Lord." Our strength fails; His never does (Isaiah 40:29–31). Our power is limited; His is eternal (Psalm 62:11).

2.2 The Whole Armour

We are commanded to put on the whole armour of God (vv. 11, 13). Partial obedience leaves us exposed. Like a soldier, we must be fully equipped every day.

3. The Armour of God

Paul paints a vivid picture of a Roman soldier, comparing his armour to the spiritual equipment God gives believers.

3.1 The Belt of Truth (v. 14)

- A Roman soldier's belt held the rest of the armour in place.
- Truth secures us. Without truth, everything else falls apart.
- Jesus is the Truth (John 14:6). God's Word is truth (John 17:17).

Application: Embrace God's truth. Reject lies, compromise, and deception.

3.2 The Breastplate of Righteousness (v. 14)

- Protects the heart — the center of life.
- Righteousness shields us from guilt, accusation, and sin.
- Christ's righteousness is our covering (2 Corinthians 5:21).

Application: Live in holiness. Guard your heart from bitterness, lust, and pride, and other sins.

3.3 The Shoes of the Gospel of Peace (v. 15)

- Roman soldiers wore boots for stability and mobility.
- The gospel gives us firm footing and readiness to move.
- We are called to carry peace and good news to others (Isaiah 52:7).

Application: Share Christ daily — with words, actions, and lifestyle.

3.4 The Shield of Faith (v. 16)

- A large Roman shield covered the entire body.
- Faith extinguishes Satan's fiery darts: doubts, fears, temptations, accusations.
- Faith is trust in God's promises (Hebrews 11:1, 6).

Application: Strengthen your faith through prayer, the Word, and testimonies of God's faithfulness.

3.5 The Helmet of Salvation (v. 17)

- Protects the head — the mind and thoughts.
- Assurance of salvation keeps us from fear and confusion.
- Salvation is both present (forgiveness) and future (eternal hope).

Application: Renew your mind daily with God's Word (Romans 12:2). Remember you are saved, secure, and sealed in Christ.

3.6 The Sword of the Spirit – The Word of God (v. 17)

- The Bible is our offensive weapon.
- Jesus defeated Satan with Scripture (Matthew 4:1–11).
- The Word is alive, powerful, and sharper than any sword (Hebrews 4:12).

Application: Memorize Scripture. Use it in prayer. Speak it against temptation.

3.7 Praying in the Spirit (v. 18)

- Prayer activates the armour.
- We are commanded to pray always — in the Spirit, with persistence.
- Prayer is both communication with God and warfare against the enemy.

Application: Develop a lifestyle of constant prayer. Pray in the Spirit (Romans 8:26–27).

3.8 Watchfulness and Perseverance (v. 18)

- Soldiers must stay alert at all times.
- Spiritual watchfulness protects against surprise attacks (1 Peter 5:8).
- Perseverance ensures we don't give up in battle.

Application: Be spiritually awake. Guard your heart, home, and church with vigilance.

3.9 Intercession for All Saints (v. 18)

- Soldiers defend each other.
- Christians must pray for one another, carrying each other's burdens (Galatians 6:2).
- Unity in prayer strengthens the whole body of Christ.

Application: Pray regularly for your family, church, leaders, missionaries, and persecuted believers.

4. Living in Victory

- We don't fight for victory; we fight from victory — Christ has already won (Colossians 2:15).
- But we must enforce that victory daily by wearing God's armour.
- Strength comes not from striving, but from abiding in Christ (John 15:4–5).

Interactive Q&A

Q1: Why is spiritual warfare real for every believer?
A1: Because Satan seeks to deceive, discourage, divide, and destroy (1 Peter 5:8).

Q2: What does the "whole armour of God" mean?
A2: Complete dependence on God's truth, righteousness, gospel, faith, salvation, Word, prayer, vigilance, and intercession.

Q3: Why is truth called the belt?
A3: Because it holds everything together — without truth, all else collapses.

Q4: Which piece of armour do you personally need to strengthen most?
A4: (Personal reflection — answers may vary).

Q5: How can prayer and watchfulness keep the armour active?
A5: Prayer brings God's power into the fight; watchfulness keeps us alert to Satan's schemes.

Reflection Points

- Do I wear God's armour daily, or only in crisis?
- Which piece of the armour do I often neglect?
- Do I see spiritual warfare in my daily struggles, or do I misidentify the enemy?
- How can I strengthen my prayer and intercession life this week?

Closing Prayer

Lord, thank You for giving us the armour of God. Forgive me for the times I relied on my own strength. Help me daily to wear the belt of truth, breastplate of righteousness, gospel shoes, shield of faith, helmet of salvation, and the sword of the Spirit. Teach me to pray, to watch, and to intercede for others. Strengthen me to stand firm and live in the victory Christ has already won. In Jesus' name, Amen.

Chapter 7

The Great Commission and Soul Winning

(Matthew 28:19–20)

"Go ye therefore, and teach all nations, baptizing them in the name of the Father, and of the Son, and of the Holy Ghost: Teaching them to observe all things whatsoever I have commanded you: and, lo, I am with you alway, even unto the end of the world." (Matthew 28:19–20)

Introduction

The heartbeat of heaven is souls. From Genesis to Revelation, God's mission has always been redemption —

bringing men and women back into fellowship with Him. When Jesus gave His final command before ascending into heaven, He did not tell His disciples to build empires, but to make disciples. The Great Commission is not a suggestion; it is a command. Every believer is called to be a witness. You may not stand on a pulpit, but your life, words, and love can draw others to Christ. Evangelism is not an event — it is a lifestyle of shining Christ's light in everyday life. Jesus said, 'Follow Me, and I will make you fishers of men' (Matthew 4:19). Following Christ naturally leads to fishing for souls. When we stop winning souls, we stop following fully.

The Mandate of the Great Commission

The Great Commission is God's global mission entrusted to His church. It has three key instructions:

• Go — We must take the gospel beyond the church walls.

• Teach (Make Disciples) — Evangelism is more than conversion; it's transformation through teaching.

• Baptize — To establish new believers in the family of faith through public confession and fellowship.

Jesus didn't say, 'Sit and wait for them to come.' He said, 'Go!' This means every believer is sent. Whether in your office, market, classroom, or home, you are God's ambassador (2 Corinthians 5:20).

Why Soul Winning Matters

• It is the Father's Desire — God 'is not willing that any should perish, but that all should come to repentance' (2 Peter 3:9).

• It was Jesus' Mission — 'The Son of Man is come to seek and to save that which was lost' (Luke 19:10).

• It is the Church's Assignment — Every sermon, service, and ministry exists to save souls.

• It is the Measure of True Love — If we truly love God and people, we will care for their eternal destiny.

• It brings Heavenly Joy — 'There is joy in the presence of the angels of God over one sinner that repenteth' (Luke 15:10).

Equipping for Evangelism: Love and Wisdom

Evangelism without love becomes argument. Evangelism without wisdom becomes offense. The gospel must be shared with both.

1. Love as the Motivation — You cannot win people you don't love. Jesus was moved with compassion before He healed or preached. Real soul winning begins when you see people as God sees them — broken but redeemable. Love disarms resistance and opens hearts.

2. Wisdom as the Method — Proverbs 11:30 says, 'He that winneth souls is wise.' Wisdom is knowing how to reach people where they are. To the intellectual, you reason with Scripture; to the hurting, you offer compassion; to the skeptic, you show consistency; to the lost, you demonstrate truth through love. Be sensitive to the Holy Spirit — He knows what each heart needs.

The Power Behind Soul Winning

We are not called to win souls by our own strength but by the power of the Holy Spirit. Acts 1:8 says, 'But ye shall receive power, after that the Holy Ghost is come upon you: and ye shall be witnesses unto me...' The Holy Spirit gives courage to speak, wisdom to answer, and anointing to convict hearts. Without Him, evangelism becomes dry persuasion. With Him, it becomes life-changing revelation.

Methods of Evangelism

• Personal Evangelism — One-on-one sharing of your faith (John 4:7–29).

• Lifestyle Evangelism — Living in a way that reflects Christ daily (Matthew 5:16).

• Public Evangelism — Street outreach, crusades, and open-air preaching.

- Digital Evangelism — Using social media, videos, and online platforms to share the gospel.

- Intercessory Evangelism — Winning souls through prayer and spiritual warfare.

Rewards of Soul Winning

- Heavenly Joy and Celebration (Luke 15:10).

- Divine Honour and Glory (Daniel 12:3 — 'They that turn many to righteousness shall shine as the stars for ever and ever.').

- Answered Prayers — Soul winners align with God's heartbeat, and He backs their requests.

- Eternal Crown — There is a special crown of rejoicing reserved for soul winners (1 Thessalonians 2:19).

- Kingdom Partnership — Every soul saved through you adds fruit to your spiritual account (Philippians 4:17).

Practical Ways to Begin

- Share your testimony — it's your most powerful sermon.

- Carry gospel tracts or digital cards wherever you go.

- Invite someone to church or a Bible study.

- Support missions financially and in prayer.

- Be available for the Spirit's prompting — sometimes, one conversation can save a life.

Interactive Q&A

Q1: Who gave the Great Commission and to whom?
A1: Jesus gave it to all believers — not just pastors or missionaries (Matthew 28:19–20).

Q2: What is the true goal of soul winning?
A2: Not just decisions for Christ, but disciples who grow in faith and obedience.

Q3: How can I overcome fear in evangelism?
A3: By relying on the Holy Spirit, remembering that it's God who saves — you are only His vessel (Acts 1:8).

Q4: What is the most powerful tool in soul winning?
A4: Love. People may argue with doctrine, but they cannot deny genuine love and compassion.

Q5: What reward awaits soul winners?
A5: Eternal joy, divine favour, answered prayers, and the crown of rejoicing (Daniel 12:3; 1 Thessalonians 2:19).

Reflection Points

- Do I see evangelism as a command or an option?
- Who in my life needs to hear the gospel from me?
- How can I use my gifts or profession for soul winning?
- Am I partnering with the Holy Spirit daily in this mission?
- When last did I lead someone to Christ or pray for the lost?

Closing Prayer

Lord Jesus, thank You for calling me to be Your witness. Fill me with love for souls and wisdom to reach them. Remove fear and give me boldness through the Holy Spirit. Let my life, words, and actions draw people to You. Use me as a vessel of salvation in my generation. May I never lose the passion for the lost. In Jesus' name, Amen.

Chapter 8

Giving in the New Testament
(Matthew 10:8; 1 Corinthians 16:2–3; Luke 6:38; 2 Corinthians 9:6–8; Exodus 23:15)

> "Heal the sick, cleanse the lepers, raise the dead, cast out devils: freely ye have received, freely give" (Matthew 10:8).
> "Give, and it shall be given unto you; good measure, pressed down, and shaken together, and running over ..." (Luke 6:38).
> "He which soweth sparingly shall reap also sparingly ... God loveth a cheerful giver" (2 Corinthians 9:6–7).
> "None shall appear before Me empty-handed" (Exodus 23:15; Deuteronomy 16:16–17).

Introduction

Giving is at the heart of the Christian life, because God Himself is a giver. He gave His only Son, and through Him freely gives us all things. In the Old Testament, giving was structured under the law, but in the New Testament it flows from grace and gratitude. Jesus reminds us: "Freely you have received, freely give." True giving goes beyond money; it is a lifestyle of generosity that reflects the character of God. This chapter explores why and how believers are called to give joyfully and sacrificially.

The Spirit of New Testament Giving

The foundation of New Testament giving is freedom and love. Jesus commanded: "Freely you have received, freely give" (Matthew 10:8). Grace itself is God's greatest gift — unearned, undeserved, freely given. Our giving is simply a response to God's generosity.

Unlike the Old Testament tithe — a compulsory 10% — New Testament giving is voluntary, joyful, proportional, and sacrificial. Giving is not about rules, but about the overflow of a grateful heart.

Tithing and the Law Fulfilled

The Old Testament tithe was part of Israel's ceremonial law (Hebrews 7:5). It was agricultural, not monetary. It was tied to the Levitical priesthood. But in Christ, the law was fulfilled (Galatians 3:13).

This does not mean Christians give nothing. Instead, the bar is raised: we give not less, but more — not by compulsion, but by love. A Christian who loves God will never ask, "How little can I give?" but "How much can I bless?"

Beyond Money: A Lifestyle of Giving

New Testament giving is broad and holistic. It includes:
- Finances – supporting the church, missions, and the poor (Philippians 4:15–19).
- Time – serving in ministry and caring for others.
- Hospitality – opening our homes and hearts (Romans 12:13; Hebrews 13:2).
- Encouragement – giving words of life (Ephesians 4:29).
- Care and compassion – visiting the sick, clothing the naked (Matthew 25:35–36).

Paul describes the Macedonian believers: "In a great trial of affliction the abundance of their joy and their deep poverty abounded unto the riches of their liberality" (2 Corinthians 8:2).

Giving as Worship

Giving is not merely financial support; it is worship. Paul calls the Philippians' financial gift "an odour of a sweet smell, a sacrifice acceptable, well-pleasing to God" (Philippians 4:18).

Every offering we bring — whether time, service, or money — is an act of worship, saying: "Lord, You are worthy of all I have." That is why Scripture says, "None shall appear before Me empty-handed" (Exodus 23:15).

Giving as Fellowship and Partnership

Paul often spoke of giving as partnership in the gospel. The Philippians shared with him in giving and receiving (Philippians 4:15). The Corinthians were urged to join in supporting the Jerusalem believers (1 Corinthians 16:1–3).

When we give, we are not just supporting an organization; we are partnering with God's Kingdom mission on earth.

The Rewards of Giving

The Bible is clear: giving carries reward.
- On earth – God promises sufficiency and abundance (2 Corinthians 9:8).
- In heaven – we lay up treasures where moth and rust cannot destroy (Matthew 6:19–21).
- In others – we bless lives, strengthen the church, and glorify God.

Jesus Himself said, "It is more blessed to give than to receive" (Acts 20:35).

Barriers to Giving

Many Christians struggle with giving because of:
- Fear of lack – forgetting God is Provider.
- Selfishness – clinging tightly instead of sowing generously.
- Misunderstanding – thinking giving is only about money.
- Legalism – giving out of guilt instead of love.

But faith teaches us that generosity never leads to lack. "There is that scattereth, and yet increaseth ..." (Proverbs 11:24).

Interactive Q&A

Q1: Why is giving in the New Testament different from Old Testament tithing?
A1: Because tithing was part of the law, while Christians are under grace. We give freely, cheerfully, and proportionally (2 Corinthians 9:7).

Q2: What are some non-financial ways Christians can give?
A2: Time, hospitality, encouragement, prayer, love, compassion, service, and care for the needy (Romans 12:13; Galatians 6:10).

Q3: How is giving an act of worship?
A3: Every offering is a sacrifice pleasing to God (Philippians 4:18). Giving declares God's worth.

Q4: What rewards does Scripture attach to giving?
A4: Earthly sufficiency (2 Corinthians 9:8), heavenly treasure (Matthew 6:19–21), and blessings to others (Acts 20:35).

Q5: Why do some Christians find it hard to give?
A5: Fear of lack, selfishness, misunderstanding, or legalism. But God's Word teaches that generosity brings increase (Proverbs 11:24).

Reflection Points

- Do I see giving as worship, or just financial obligation?
- Am I bringing something whenever I appear before God, or am I "empty-handed"?
- In what ways can I expand my giving beyond money?
- Do I trust God as my Provider when I give generously?
- Am I giving cheerfully, or grudgingly?

Closing Prayer

Heavenly Father, thank You for the gift of salvation and every blessing You freely give. Forgive me for times I held back in fear or selfishness. Teach me to see giving as worship, as partnership, and as love in action. Help me to give generously of my resources, my time, my love, and my service. May I never appear before You empty-handed, but may my life overflow with cheerful generosity that glorifies Your name. In Jesus' name, Amen.

Chapter 9

Greed: The Silent Enemy of the Soul

(Luke 12:15)

"And He said unto them, Take heed, and beware of covetousness: for a man's life consisteth not in the abundance of the things which he possesseth." (Luke 12:15)

Introduction

Greed is one of the most deceptive sins because it rarely appears dangerous on the surface. It can disguise itself as ambition, careful planning, or the desire for security. Yet

Jesus warned that life does not consist in the abundance of possessions. Greed enslaves the heart, blinds the soul, and destroys both individuals and communities. From Achan to Judas, the Bible shows how greed leads only to ruin. This chapter exposes the danger of covetousness and shows the freedom found in contentment and generosity.

Understanding Greed: More Than Just Desire

Greed is not simply wanting something — it is a restless craving that refuses to be satisfied. The Greek word for covetousness (pleonexia) means "the desire to have more." Greed whispers, "What I have is never enough; I must have more." It often hides beneath ambition, thrift, or even prudence, but its fruit always reveals bondage rather than freedom.

Greed is not only about money. It can manifest as:
- Greed for wealth — hoarding money at the expense of generosity.
- Greed for power — craving control or recognition above others.
- Greed for pleasure — a restless pursuit of self-indulgence.
- Greed for things — consumerism that equates worth with possessions.

Greed in the Bible: Lessons of Ruin

Scripture shows that greed destroys those who indulge in it:

- Achan's Greed (Joshua 7:20–25): Achan secretly took forbidden treasures. His sin led to Israel's defeat in battle and cost his family their lives.
- Gehazi's Greed (2 Kings 5:20–27): Gehazi lied to Naaman to gain wealth. His greed brought leprosy upon him and his descendants.
- Judas's Greed (Matthew 26:14–15): For thirty pieces of silver, Judas betrayed the Son of God, sealing his eternal tragedy.

Greed always promises gain but delivers destruction.

Why Greed Is Spiritual Idolatry

Paul warns: "No covetous man, who is an idolater, hath any inheritance in the kingdom of Christ and of God" (Ephesians 5:5). Greed is idolatry because it replaces God with possessions.

Idols in ancient times were carved images. Idols today are often hidden in the heart: a bank balance, a career, or a lifestyle that we cannot let go of. The greedy heart bows to these idols instead of to Christ.

Greed Versus Contentment

Greed and contentment cannot dwell in the same heart. Hebrews 13:5 commands: "Let your conversation be without covetousness; and be content with such things as ye have."

- Contentment trusts God's promises.
- Greed doubts God's provision.
- Contentment says, "God is enough."
- Greed says, "God has not given me enough."

Paul testified: "I have learned, in whatsoever state I am, therewith to be content" (Philippians 4:11). True wealth is not measured in possessions, but in peace.

How Greed Harms Others

Greed is never harmless. It spreads corruption and injustice:

- The prophets condemned those who exploited the poor (Amos 8:4–6).
- Isaiah cried against leaders who added house to house and field to field, leaving none for others (Isaiah 5:8).
- In our world today, greed fuels corruption, human trafficking, environmental destruction, and economic inequality.

A greedy person never sins alone — families, churches, and communities feel the ripple effects.

The Eternal Danger of Greed

Jesus asked: "For what shall it profit a man, if he shall gain the whole world, and lose his own soul?" (Mark 8:36). Greed blinds us to eternity, causing us to trade heavenly treasure for earthly dust.

The rich fool in Luke 12:16–21 built bigger barns but lost his soul in a single night. His wealth could not follow him into eternity. Similarly, greed blinds modern Christians from investing in what truly lasts: eternal souls, Kingdom work, and the treasures of heaven.

Overcoming Greed: Practical Steps

Greed can be defeated by cultivating generosity and contentment:

1. Practice Gratitude — regularly thank God for what you already have (1 Thessalonians 5:18).
2. Set Eternal Priorities — seek first the Kingdom of God (Matthew 6:33).
3. Give Generously — generosity breaks greed's grip (Acts 20:35).

4. Avoid Comparison — envy fuels greed; fix your eyes on Christ (2 Corinthians 10:12).

5. Live Simply — choose lifestyle over luxury, purpose over possessions (1 Timothy 6:6–8).

Interactive Q&A

Q1: How did Jesus warn against greed in Luke 12:15?
A1: By teaching that life is not measured by possessions but by relationship with God.

Q2: Give two biblical examples of greed and their consequences.
A2: Achan (Joshua 7:20–25) and Judas (Matthew 26:14–15) — both ended in destruction.

Q3: Why does Paul call greed idolatry (Ephesians 5:5)?
A3: Because greed puts wealth or possessions in the place of God.

Q4: What is the biblical antidote to greed?
A4: Contentment and trust in God's provision (Hebrews 13:5; Philippians 4:19).

Q5: How does greed harm others?
A5: It leads to oppression, corruption, and injustice, affecting families, communities, and society at large (Amos 8:4–6).

Reflection Points

- Am I pursuing possessions more than I pursue Christ?
- Do I believe God's provision is truly enough for me?
- In what ways might I be turning money or success into an idol?
- How can I practice generosity this week to break greed's power?
- Where am I storing treasure — on earth, or in heaven?

Closing Prayer

Father in heaven, thank You for reminding me that true life does not consist in possessions, but in knowing You. Forgive me for times I have allowed greed, fear, or comparison to rule my heart. Teach me to live in contentment, to trust Your provision, and to treasure eternal riches above earthly gain. Fill me with a generous spirit that reflects Your love. In Jesus' name, Amen.

Chapter 10

Be Not Drunk with Wine, But Filled with the Spirit
(Ephesians 5:18; Proverbs 20:1)

"Wine is a mocker, strong drink is raging: and whosoever is deceived thereby is not wise." (Proverbs 20:1)

Introduction

From the earliest pages of Scripture, God has warned His people about the dangers of losing control. Whether through anger, lust, pride, or intoxication, the enemy's strategy has always been to make humanity lose self-governance — to silence the conscience and blur spiritual sensitivity.

Ephesians 5:18 gives us both a warning and a command: "Be not drunk with wine, wherein is excess; but be filled with the Spirit." Drunkenness represents more than just physical intoxication; it symbolizes anything that dulls our spiritual senses and replaces the influence of the Holy Spirit. While the world may glorify indulgence, the believer is called to walk in discipline, clarity, and holiness.

The Bible does not merely prohibit drunkenness; it points us toward something far better — the fullness of the Holy Spirit. When the Spirit fills our hearts, He replaces the counterfeit pleasures of the flesh with divine joy, peace, and power. This chapter examines the spiritual and moral dangers of alcohol and intoxicating substances, contrasts them with the beauty of a Spirit-filled life, and calls us to live soberly, righteously, and godly in this present world (Titus 2:12).

Alcohol and Intoxicating Substances

Alcoholic drinks include wine, beer, and strong liquors. Intoxicating substances also include cigarettes, marijuana, narcotics, and any chemical that alters the mind or behaviour. To intoxicate means to lose control of one's reasoning, emotions, or actions. Scripture consistently warns that intoxication leads to sin, shame, sickness, addiction, and spiritual destruction.

Noah's Weakness — A Lesson for All

In Genesis 9:20–23, Noah — a man who had walked faithfully with God and found grace to preserve humanity — fell into weakness after the flood. He planted a vineyard, drank of the wine, became drunk, and uncovered himself within his tent. Even great men can stumble when they lose self-control. This story reminds us that God's grace does not excuse carelessness. We must learn from Noah's failure, not repeat it.

The Effects of Intoxication

- Loss of control — Noah lay exposed and vulnerable.
- Broken family honour — Ham mocked his father's shame, while Shem and Japheth grieved.
- Hasty speech — Noah's words of anger brought unnecessary curses.
- Disgrace — What began with pleasure ended in humiliation.

This same pattern plays out today: drunkenness and substance abuse lead to disease, poverty, immorality, broken homes, and spiritual decay.

What the Bible Says About Alcohol

- Proverbs 31:4–5 — It is not for kings to drink wine, lest they forget the law and pervert judgment.

- Proverbs 20:1 — Wine is a mocker, strong drink is raging: and whosoever is deceived thereby is not wise.

- Proverbs 23:20–21 — Be not among winebibbers… for the drunkard and the glutton shall come to poverty.

- 1 Peter 5:8 — Be sober, be vigilant; because your adversary the devil walketh about seeking whom he may devour.

Intoxication weakens our vigilance and dulls spiritual alertness — the very qualities we need to resist temptation and discern the will of God.

The Bible's Balance

The Bible does not call wine itself a sin. In 1 Timothy 5:23, Paul advised Timothy to use a little wine for medicinal purposes. The sin lies not in the substance, but in the excess that leads to loss of control. When Scripture says, "Be not drunk with wine," it warns against surrendering the heart to anything that competes with the Holy Spirit's control.

The Christian Witness

As followers of Christ, we are called to be the light of the world (Matthew 5:14–16). How can light shine brightly if it is dimmed by indulgence? A believer enslaved by alcohol or drugs cannot effectively represent the holiness and freedom found in Christ. Abstaining from intoxicants is not legalism — it is testimony. It says to the world, "My joy and peace come not from a bottle, but from the Spirit of God."

The Alternative: Filled with the Spirit

Ephesians 5:18 offers a glorious alternative: "Be filled with the Spirit." Where alcohol dulls the senses, the Holy Spirit awakens them. Where wine brings temporary laughter, the Spirit brings eternal joy. To be filled with the Spirit is to live under divine influence — controlled not by emotion, but by God's presence and power.

Interactive Q&A

Q1: What are alcoholic drinks and intoxicating substances?
A1: They are substances like wine, strong drink, cigarettes, drugs, or narcotics that intoxicate and impair self-control.

Q2: What are their effects?
A2: They lead to shame, sickness, addiction, poverty, confusion, and loss of dignity.

Q3: Should Christians consume them?
A3: Scripture warns against drunkenness and indulgence. Believers are called to sobriety, vigilance, and holiness.

Q4: What should Christians be filled with instead of alcohol?
A4: The Holy Spirit, who produces joy, wisdom, strength, and godly character (Ephesians 5:18; Galatians 5:22–23).

Q5: How does abstaining from intoxicants strengthen Christian witness?
A5: A sober and Spirit-filled life preserves a believer's testimony, inspires others, and sets an example of holiness.

Reflection Points

- Am I allowing any habit or substance to control me instead of the Holy Spirit?
- Do my choices strengthen or weaken my witness for Christ?
- How can I help those trapped in addiction find freedom in Christ?
- Do I treasure the fruit of the Spirit more than the fleeting pleasures of the flesh?

Closing Prayer

Lord, thank You for the clarity of Your Word and the warning it gives. Forgive me for any moment when I allowed something other than Your Spirit to control me. Fill me afresh with Your Holy Spirit — with wisdom, purity, and joy. Help me to live soberly and to shine as a light to others who are struggling. Let my life glorify You in every choice I make. In Jesus' name, Amen.

Chapter 11

Pride: The Hidden Destroyer
(Proverbs 16:18)

"Pride goeth before destruction, and an haughty spirit before a fall." (Proverbs 16:18)

Introduction

Pride is a hidden destroyer — a sin that often disguises itself as confidence, self-worth, or strength, yet beneath it lies rebellion against God and contempt toward others. It was pride that cast Lucifer from heaven, pride that deceived Adam and Eve in the Garden, and pride that continues to break families, churches, and nations today. Unlike outward sins that are visible to all, pride lurks in the heart, poisoning thoughts, words, and actions until it finally brings ruin.

The Bible warns against pride more than once because it is subtle, dangerous, and universal. Whether it is pride toward God in self-sufficiency, or pride toward man in arrogance and superiority, the result is the same: destruction. Humility, by contrast, opens the door to grace, peace, and restored fellowship with both God and people.

The Nature of Pride

Pride is one of the most dangerous sins, because it attacks in two directions:
- Against God — refusing to depend on Him, exalting self above His will.
- Against people — despising others, looking down on them, and treating them as less worthy.

It is more than arrogance in words or actions; it is an inward posture of the heart that exalts self above both God and fellow man. Scripture calls pride sin because it blinds us to our need for grace (Proverbs 21:4) and poisons our relationships.

Pride in the Beginning

From the start, pride brought destruction:
- Lucifer's Pride: He exalted himself against God's throne (Isaiah 14:13–14).
- Eden's Pride: Adam and Eve believed they could be "as gods" (Genesis 3:5).
- Human Pride Today: People often set themselves above others — in wealth, position, talent, or race. But all pride has the same root: rebellion against God's order of humility and love.

The Fruit of Pride Toward God and Man

Pride always ends in downfall:
- Before God: Nebuchadnezzar was humbled until he confessed God's greatness (Daniel 4:30–34).
- Before Man: The Pharisee in Luke 18:10–14 looked down on the tax collector, boasting of his own righteousness. Yet the humble tax collector was justified.

Pride ruins our fellowship with God and destroys unity with others.

Why God Hates Pride

James 4:6 says, "God resisteth the proud, but giveth grace unto the humble."

- Pride toward God robs Him of His glory.
- Pride toward people denies the truth that all men are equal before Him.

When we despise others — because of their background, education, social status, or even spiritual maturity — we forget that Christ died equally for all. Pride breaks the law of love (1 Corinthians 13:4–5).

The Call to Humility Toward God and People

The antidote to pride is humility, shown in two ways:
- Before God: "Humble yourselves under the mighty hand of God" (1 Peter 5:6).
- Before people: "Let nothing be done through strife or vainglory; but in lowliness of mind let each esteem other better than themselves" (Philippians 2:3).

Jesus modeled both. He humbled Himself before the Father's will (Philippians 2:8) and washed His disciples' feet (John 13:14–15). Humility toward God leads us to dependence; humility toward people leads us to service.

Overcoming Pride in Daily Life

Pride is defeated when we actively practice humility:

1. Submit to God in all things (James 4:7).
2. Acknowledge others' worth — treat people with respect and kindness (Romans 12:10).
3. Imitate Christ's humility (Philippians 2:5–8).
4. Practice gratitude — remembering all we have is a gift (1 Corinthians 4:7).
5. Serve others in love — humility is not just an attitude but an action (Galatians 5:13).
6. Guard against arrogance — avoid boasting, comparing, or despising others (Luke 14:11).

Interactive Q&A

Q1: What is pride according to the Bible?
A1: Pride is a heart lifted against God and an attitude of arrogance toward others (Proverbs 21:4).

Q2: Why does God resist the proud?
A2: Because pride rejects dependence on Him and despises people made in His image (James 4:6).

Q3: Give an example of pride leading to destruction.
A3: Lucifer's fall from heaven (Isaiah 14:12–15), Nebuchadnezzar's humiliation (Daniel 4:30–33), and the Pharisee who exalted himself while despising others (Luke 18:11–14).

Q4: What is the opposite of pride, and how is it expressed?

A4: Humility. Before God, it means submission; before people, it means service and respect (1 Peter 5:6; Philippians 2:3).

Q5: How can believers overcome pride in daily life?
A5: By submitting to God, valuing others above themselves, imitating Christ's humility, practicing gratitude, and serving others in love (Philippians 2:3–5).

Reflection Points

- Do I secretly think of myself as better than others in any area?
- How do I respond when corrected by God or people?
- Do I find it difficult to serve those "beneath" me?
- Have I ever robbed God of glory by boasting in my own strength?
- What step of humility can I take today — toward God and toward others?

Closing Prayer

Lord, search my heart and expose every trace of pride. Forgive me for the times I exalted myself above You or looked down on others. Teach me to walk in humility before You, depending on Your grace, and in gentleness toward people, esteeming them better than myself. Let the mind of Christ, full of humility and love, rule in me. In Jesus' name, Amen

Chapter 12

Faith in Action – Closing the Gap Between Knowing and Doing
(James 1:22)

"But be ye doers of the word, and not hearers only, deceiving your own selves."
(James 1:22)

Introduction

Life is not changed by what we know, but by what we do with what we know. Many people grow old with libraries of knowledge in their heads but very little fruit in their lives, because they never moved from hearing to doing.

Procrastination, delay, laziness, and fear steal time until years slip away and regret takes their place.

This truth applies not only to our walk with God, but also to our families, careers, studies, finances, and every area of personal growth. A student may know how to study but fail to prepare; a worker may know how to improve but never apply it; a believer may know God's Word yet fail to act on it. Success — both spiritual and practical — is not in knowing alone, but in doing.

Knowledge Without Action Is Deception

Spiritually, James warns us not to deceive ourselves by hearing only (James 1:22). Practically, we deceive ourselves when we plan endlessly but never execute. Vision without action is daydreaming. Jesus said the wise man is the one who hears and does, building on the rock (Matthew 7:24–27). Knowledge is potential, but action is power.

The Danger of Procrastination

Procrastination delays destiny. Spiritually: Felix told Paul, "Go thy way for now; when I have a convenient season, I will call for thee" (Acts 24:25). That convenient season never came. Practically: Many delay starting a business, pursuing education, or reconciling relationships — until it is too late. Scripture warns: "He that observeth the wind shall not sow; and he that regardeth the clouds shall not reap" (Ecclesiastes 11:4). Waiting for "perfect conditions" leads to wasted seasons.

Laziness and the Poverty of Inaction

The Bible says: "The soul of the sluggard desireth, and hath nothing: but the soul of the diligent shall be made fat" (Proverbs 13:4). Desire without diligence leads to emptiness. In work: Laziness kills productivity, leaving dreams unfulfilled. In family: Failing to invest time in loved ones results in regret later. In finances: Failing to budget, save, or invest results in perpetual lack. Laziness is not only physical idleness but also the habit of postponing, avoiding, and excusing.

Fear: The Silent Paralyzer

Another reason people fail to act is fear.
- Fear of the unknown: Israel stood on the edge of the Promised Land, but fear of giants kept them from entering (Numbers 13:31–33).
- Fear of failure: Many hesitate to start new ventures because they fear making mistakes, yet God says, "Fear thou not; for I am with thee" (Isaiah 41:10).
- Fear of rejection: Some never share the gospel, apply for

opportunities, or step out in faith because they dread being turned away.

Fear is natural, but it should never rule us. "God hath not given us the spirit of fear; but of power, and of love, and of a sound mind" (2 Timothy 1:7). Acting in faith means trusting God beyond our comfort zone.

The Blessing of Immediate Obedience

God blesses swift obedience. Spiritually: Abraham obeyed immediately when God called him (Genesis 12:4). The disciples left their nets at once (Mark 1:18). The Philippian jailer, upon hearing the gospel, was baptized the same night (Acts 16:33). Practically: Those who act on their vision quickly create opportunities. Many world changers were not the most knowledgeable, but the most decisive. Obedience — both to God's Word and to life's responsibilities — multiplies results.

Doing Produces the Harvest

"If ye know these things, happy are ye if ye do them" (John 13:17). Joy is in doing. Farmers who never plant never reap. Likewise, people who never apply principles of health, work, or study reap frustration instead of fruit. Galatians 6:7 teaches that sowing brings reaping. The same applies to sowing effort in career, marriage, ministry, or personal growth.

Practical Keys to Closing the Gap

1. Start Now — Stop waiting for perfect conditions; act today (Ecclesiastes 11:4).
2. Break Goals Into Steps — Large visions become manageable when divided into daily actions (Habakkuk 2:2).
3. Discipline the Body and Mind — Paul said, "I keep under my body, and bring it into subjection" (1 Corinthians 9:27).
4. Eliminate Excuses — Replace "I will do it later" with "I will do it now" (Proverbs 6:9–11).
5. Confront Fear With Faith — Step out trusting God's promises; He is greater than any unknown (Isaiah 41:10).
6. Accountability — Share your goals with trusted people who will challenge you (Proverbs 27:17).
7. Balance Spiritual and Practical — Pray, but also plan; believe, but also build; know God's Word, but also apply it in career, family, and finances.

Interactive Q&A

Q1: Why is knowledge without action dangerous?
A1: Because it deceives us into thinking we are growing, while in truth only action produces fruit (James 1:22; Matthew

7:24–27).

Q2: How does procrastination rob people of success?
A2: It delays obedience and productivity, wasting time and opportunities (Acts 24:25; Ecclesiastes 11:4).

Q3: What role does fear play in stopping people from acting?
A3: Fear of the unknown, failure, or rejection keeps many from stepping into God's best — but He has given us power, love, and a sound mind (2 Timothy 1:7).

Q4: Give examples of immediate obedience that brought blessing.
A4: Abraham obeyed immediately when God called him (Genesis 12:4), and the disciples followed Jesus without delay (Mark 1:18).

Q5: How can believers apply this principle beyond spiritual life?
A5: By taking consistent action in work, family, finances, studies, and personal growth — not just hearing but doing in all areas of life (Luke 16:10; 2 Timothy 1:7).

Reflection Points

- What areas of my life show knowledge but no action — spiritually, financially, or relationally?
- Do I use procrastination as an excuse to avoid responsibility?
- How has delay, laziness, or fear of the unknown affected my career, studies, or ministry?
- What one step of immediate obedience can I take today — despite fear — in my walk with God, in my work, or in my family?

Closing Prayer

Heavenly Father, thank You for reminding me that true success comes not only from knowing, but from doing. Forgive me for the times I delayed, procrastinated, or let fear stop me. Break the chains of fear in my life, and fill me with boldness to step into the unknown with faith in Your promises. Help me to act with diligence in every area — spiritually, practically, and relationally — so my life may bear lasting fruit for Your glory. In Jesus' name, Amen.

Chapter 13

Fear Not – Living in Courage and Faith
(Matthew 10:26–28)

> *"Fear them not therefore: for there is nothing covered, that shall not be revealed; and hid, that shall not be known... And fear not them which kill the body, but are not able to kill the soul: but rather fear Him which is able to destroy both soul and body in hell." (Matthew 10:26, 28)*

Introduction

Fear is one of the most common human emotions, yet one of the greatest enemies of faith. From Genesis to

Revelation, God repeatedly tells His people: "Fear not." It is said there are 365 "fear nots" in the Bible — one for each day of the year.

Why does God emphasize this so much? Because fear paralyzes. It blinds people to God's promises, robs them of courage, and keeps them from stepping into the fullness of His plan. Fear is not from God (2 Timothy 1:7). It is the absence of faith (Matthew 8:26). Faith and fear cannot coexist: where one thrives, the other dies.

Fear is one of the enemy's greatest weapons to destabilize the children of God. But God has given us tools to conquer fear and live by faith, courage, and confidence in Him.

The Nature of Fear

Fear is deceptive. It magnifies shadows and makes lies look like truth.
- False Experience Appearing Real (F.E.A.R.): Fear paints pictures in the mind of disasters that never happen. Most of the things we worry about never come to pass.
- Fear Weakens and Confuses: A fearful heart cannot think clearly. Fear shakes confidence and clouds judgment. A soldier or athlete ruled by fear is already half-defeated before the real battle begins.
- Fear Gives Satan a Foothold: Job, though the wealthiest man in the East, lived constantly in fear. "The thing which I greatly

feared is come upon me" (Job 3:25). His lack of peace gave the enemy an entry point.

Fear does not prevent evil; it only multiplies suffering.

Biblical Examples of Fear's Destruction

The Bible shows how fear ruins lives and destiny:
- Abraham and Isaac both lied about their wives because of fear (Genesis 12:13; 26:7).
- Jeroboam built idols because he feared losing political power (1 Kings 12:26–30).
- The ten spies feared giants and discouraged a whole nation from entering the Promised Land (Numbers 13:31–33).
- King Saul, though taller than all Israel, trembled before Goliath (1 Samuel 17:11).

Fear makes strong men weak, great men small, and faithful men disobedient. Even today, fear manifests in anxiety, worry, and stress — leading to sleeplessness, high blood pressure, and countless other health problems.

The Only Good Fear

Not all fear is destructive. There is one fear the Bible commands: the fear of the Lord.
- Jesus taught: "Fear Him which is able to destroy both soul

and body in hell" (Matthew 10:28).
- This fear is not terror, but reverence, awe, and obedience.

The fear of the Lord produces blessing, not bondage:
- It is the beginning of wisdom and knowledge (Proverbs 1:7; 9:10; Psalm 111:10).
- It is a fountain of life (Proverbs 14:27).
- It gives strong confidence (Proverbs 14:26).
- It prolongs life (Proverbs 10:27).

Unlike destructive fear, the fear of the Lord anchors us, protects us, and draws us closer to God.

Fear and Secret Sins

Jesus warned: "There is nothing covered, that shall not be revealed; and hid, that shall not be known" (Matthew 10:26).

Fear often pushes people into hiding:
- Fear of exposure makes them cover up sins.
- Fear of rejection makes them pretend to be righteous outwardly.

But God sees everything. "The eyes of the Lord are in every place, beholding the evil and the good" (Proverbs 15:3). Fear of discovery only deepens bondage. True freedom comes when we repent and walk in the light.

A believer who lives in secret sin will always live in fear. But the one who confesses and forsakes sin finds mercy (Proverbs 28:13) — and peace replaces fear.

God's Call: Fear Not

Throughout Scripture, God calls His people to courage:
- To Abraham: "Fear not, Abram: I am thy shield" (Genesis 15:1).
- To Joshua: "Be strong and of a good courage; be not afraid" (Joshua 1:9).
- To Israel: "The Lord, He it is that doth go before thee… He will not fail thee, neither forsake thee: fear not, neither be dismayed" (Deuteronomy 31:8).

Fear adds nothing good. It does not solve problems; it makes them worse. Faith, on the other hand, invites God into the situation. When we choose faith over fear, we declare: "The Lord is my light and my salvation; whom shall I fear?" (Psalm 27:1).

Overcoming Fear in Daily Life

1. Renew Your Mind with God's Word — His promises replace lies with truth (Isaiah 41:10).
2. Pray with Faith — Prayer invites God's presence, which

drives out fear (Philippians 4:6–7).

3. Confess Boldly — Speak God's Word aloud until fear is silenced (Psalm 118:6).

4. Walk in Obedience — Fear shrinks when faith is put into action (James 2:17).

5. Keep Godly Company — Surround yourself with people of faith, not fear (Proverbs 27:17).

6. Focus on God, not Giants — Like David, fix your eyes on the greatness of God, not the size of the problem (1 Samuel 17:45).

Interactive Q&A

Q1: What is the difference between fear and faith?
A1: Fear is the absence of faith, while faith is trust in God's promises. They cannot coexist (Matthew 8:26; 2 Timothy 1:7).

Q2: Should a Christian be afraid?
A2: No. Believers are called to live by faith, not fear. Fear weakens, but faith strengthens (Joshua 1:9).

Q3: What is the only kind of fear that is acceptable before God?
A3: The fear of the Lord — reverence, worship, and obedience. It leads to wisdom, blessing, and confidence (Proverbs 9:10; 14:26–27).

Q4: Should a Christian indulge in secret sin?
A4: No. Jesus said nothing hidden will remain concealed (Matthew 10:26). God sees all things, and hidden sin brings bondage and fear.

Q5: How can a believer overcome destructive fear in daily life?
A5: By trusting God's promises, confronting fear with faith, praying for courage, confessing God's Word, and walking in obedience (Isaiah 41:10; 2 Timothy 1:7).

Reflection Points

- What fears have limited my obedience or growth in God?
- Am I more controlled by fear of man than by the fear of the Lord?
- Do I carry hidden sins that produce fear instead of freedom?
- How has fear affected my health, family, or decisions?
- What step of bold faith is God asking me to take today?

Closing Prayer

Heavenly Father, I thank You because You have not given me a spirit of fear, but of power, love, and a sound mind. Forgive me for the times I allowed fear to control me. Break the hold of fear in my life, and replace it with courage and confidence in You. Teach me to walk in reverence for You alone, to reject the lies of the enemy, and to live in the freedom of faith. Help me to stand boldly in every situation, knowing You are with me and will never forsake me. In Jesus' name, Amen.

Chapter 14

Character and Integrity – The True Image
(Acts 17:2)

"And Paul, as his manner was, went in unto them, and three sabbath days reasoned with them out of the scriptures."
(Acts 17:2)

Introduction

Every believer is known not only by their words but by their manner of life. In Acts 16, Paul was beaten, imprisoned, and publicly shamed for preaching the gospel. Yet, when released, he did not retreat in fear or regret. Instead, as his manner was, he went straight back to preaching and reasoning from the Scriptures (Acts 17:2).

Your manner of life reveals your true character. Who are you when no one is watching? What do you practice consistently? What image do you present — not just on Sundays, but every day of the week? God is not looking for part-time Christians, but men and women of character and integrity who represent Christ faithfully in every setting.

What Is Character?

Character is the sum total of what you are made of — your inner qualities, your consistent attitudes, and your behaviour when no one sees you.
- Character is seen in your thoughts: "As a man thinketh in his heart, so is he" (Proverbs 23:7).
- Character is revealed in secret actions: Jesus taught that lustful thoughts alone are adultery in God's eyes (Matthew 5:28).
- Character is your true image: while people see appearances, God sees the heart (1 Samuel 16:7).

Character can be good or bad, but it cannot be neutral. Every repeated action shapes us. Our habits form our character, and our character eventually forms our destiny.

Duplicity vs. Authenticity

Many live like "chameleons," changing colours with situations:
- Holy on Sundays but worldly during the week.
- Gentle in church but harsh at home.
- Kind in public but gossiping in secret.

Such duplicity cannot please God. True Christian character must be authentic and consistent. What you are in private is who you really are. Jesus condemned hypocrisy because it wears masks and deceives people, but "God desires truth in the inward parts" (Psalm 51:6).

Integrity: The Proof of Character

Integrity is the alignment of thought, word, and deed. It means being the same everywhere and always.
- God is our model: He never changes (Malachi 3:6). He is faithful and true (James 1:17).
- Integrity builds trust: Just as we trust God because He keeps His Word, people will only trust us if our words match our actions.
- Integrity confirms character: Without integrity, good character is only pretence.

Even language reflects this truth: letters are called "characters" because they never change — A is always A.

Likewise, a Christian should always reflect Christ — in business, in family, in church, and in secret.

Breaking Free from Bad Character

Bad character does not disappear by chance; it must be confronted.
- Habits form character: Repeating sinful actions creates strongholds. Repeating righteous actions builds godly character.
- Examples of destructive habits: lying, gossiping, lust, anger, quarrelling, cheating, unforgiveness.
- Some strongholds are demonized: The devil reinforces bad habits to make them harder to break (2 Corinthians 10:4–5).

Practical Steps to Change:
1. Declare war against sin: You cannot conquer what you tolerate (Isaiah 49:25).
2. Hate evil with perfect hatred: God fights what you fight, but He will not fight what you love.
3. Replace bad habits with godly ones: Fill your life with Scripture, prayer, worship, and fellowship.
4. Renew your mind daily: "Casting down imaginations… and bringing every thought into captivity to the obedience of Christ" (2 Corinthians 10:5).
5. Use spiritual weapons: Fasting, prayer, and deliverance break stubborn, demonized habits (2 Corinthians 10:4).

The Call to Christlike Character

Paul's manner was to preach faithfully, despite persecution. Jesus' manner was to do the will of His Father, even unto death. The real question is: What will people say your manner is?

As Christians, we are called to be consistent, trustworthy, and faithful. We represent Christ to the world. Our character is our witness, and our integrity is our testimony. A Christian without integrity misrepresents Christ.

Interactive Q&A

Q1: What do you understand as character?
A1: Character is the sum total of who you are — your consistent habits, attitudes, and actions, especially when no one is watching (Proverbs 23:7).

Q2: What are types of character?
A2: Character can be good (honesty, humility, love, integrity) or bad (lying, hypocrisy, immorality, anger). There is no neutral character.

Q3: How are characters formed?
A3: Characters are formed by repeated actions and habits, whether good or bad. What we practice continually shapes who we become (Galatians 6:7–8).

Q4: What is integrity?
A4: Integrity is being the same in private and public, ensuring that words and actions match consistently. It is the foundation of trust (Malachi 3:6; Proverbs 11:3).

Q5: How can someone get out of bad character?
A5: By declaring war against it — hating it with perfect hatred and choosing to forsake it. God will not deliver anyone from what they love (Isaiah 49:25). Replace bad habits with godly ones, and renew the mind with God's Word. Strongholds can be broken through prayer, fasting, and deliverance (2 Corinthians 10:4–5).

Reflection Points

- What is my consistent manner of life — at home, at work, in church, in secret?
- Do I live one life or wear many masks?
- Are my words and actions aligned, or do I lack integrity?
- What habits am I repeating that are shaping my character?
- What strongholds must I declare war against today with God's help?

Closing Prayer

Heavenly Father, thank You for creating me in Your image. Forgive me for every bad habit, hidden sin, and lack of integrity in my life. Help me to live with true character and to reflect Christ in all I do. Give me strength to declare war against ungodly habits and to replace them with godly ones. Teach me to walk in integrity, so that my life may be a faithful witness of Your goodness and truth. In Jesus' name, Amen.

Chapter 15

The Sabbath – Christ Our True Rest

(Exodus 31:12–18)

> *"Speak thou also unto the children of Israel, saying, Verily my sabbaths ye shall keep: for it is a sign between me and you throughout your generations; that ye may know that I am the LORD that doth sanctify you." (Exodus 31:13)*

Introduction

The Sabbath has stirred much discussion across generations. For the Jews, it is the seventh day (Saturday), a covenant sign of rest. For most Christians, worship and rest are observed on the first day (Sunday).

But beyond arguments about days, the deeper truth is this: the Sabbath is not ultimately about a day, but about a Person. True Sabbath rest is found only in Jesus Christ.

The Meaning of the Sabbath

The word Sabbath comes from the Hebrew shabbath, meaning "to rest."
- God created the heavens and the earth in six days and rested on the seventh (Genesis 2:2–3).
- For Israel, the Sabbath was a sign of covenant identity with God (Exodus 31:13).
- It was also a reminder that life is more than work — that God Himself sanctifies and sustains His people.

Rest is holy because it shifts focus from human effort to divine provision.

The Shift to Sunday Worship

Why do most Christians worship on Sunday, the first day of the week?
- Christ rose on Sunday: His resurrection marked victory over sin and death (Luke 24:1–6).
- The disciples gathered on Sunday: They met to break bread and worship on the first day (John 20:19, Acts 20:7).
- The church gave offerings on Sunday: Paul instructed

believers to set aside contributions on the first day (1 Corinthians 16:2).

The principle is significant: God deserves our first — the first of our time, energy, and devotion. Sunday worship reflects giving Jesus first place in our lives.

The Law and Grace

Some insist Christians must keep Saturday Sabbath because it is part of the Ten Commandments (Exodus 20:8–11). They argue that even Jesus rested in the grave on the Sabbath.

But Scripture reveals otherwise:
- Jesus worked even on the Sabbath, declaring, "My Father is still working, and I am working" (John 5:17).
- He taught that "the Son of Man is Lord even of the Sabbath" (Mark 2:28).
- Paul warned believers not to let anyone judge them concerning Sabbaths (Colossians 2:16).

Christ fulfilled the law. Believers are no longer under the old covenant of the letter but under the new covenant of grace (Romans 6:14; Galatians 3:13). The Sabbath command pointed to Christ, who is our eternal rest.

Rest in Christ

God designed rest for human good:
- Physical rest renews the body.
- Spiritual rest renews the soul.

But true and eternal rest cannot be found in a day; it can only be found in Christ. Jesus invites us: "Come unto me, all ye that labour and are heavy laden, and I will give you rest" (Matthew 11:28).

This rest is not laziness but refreshment in God's presence. It is freedom from striving to earn salvation, for Christ has finished the work on the cross (John 19:30). To reject rest in Christ is to remain restless, always striving but never satisfied.

The Call to Fellowship

While Christ is our rest, Scripture still calls us to gather as His people. Hebrews 10:25 warns against neglecting fellowship. Worshiping with other believers is not optional — it strengthens faith, provides encouragement, and glorifies God.

Staying home out of convenience or busyness misses the purpose of both Sabbath and Sunday gatherings: to rest in God and to build His people.

Interactive Q&A

Q1: What is the Sabbath, and what does it mean?
A1: The Sabbath means "rest." In the Old Testament, it was the seventh day (Saturday), given as a covenant sign of God's sanctifying power (Exodus 31:13; Genesis 2:2–3).

Q2: Why do most Christians worship on Sunday?
A2: Because Christ rose on Sunday, the first day of the week. The early church gathered, gave offerings, and broke bread on Sunday to honour His resurrection (John 20:19; 1 Corinthians 16:2).

Q3: What does it mean that Christians are not under the law but under grace?
A3: It means we are saved by Christ's finished work, not by keeping ceremonial laws (Romans 6:14). Grace does not give license to sin but empowers us to walk by the Spirit (Galatians 5:16–25).

Q4: What guides New Testament believers if not the law?
A4: Believers are guided by the Holy Spirit. He leads us to avoid works of the flesh and to bear the fruit of the Spirit (Galatians 5:22–23).

Q5: Where can one find true rest, and how long does it last?
A5: True rest is found only in Christ, who is Lord of the Sabbath (Matthew 12:8). His rest is eternal — beginning now in salvation and continuing forever in His presence (Hebrews 4:9–10).

Reflection Points

- Do I see the Sabbath as just a day, or as an invitation to rest in Christ?
- Do I give God the first place in my time and devotion?
- Am I living in grace, or am I still bound by legalism?
- Do I regularly gather with God's people to strengthen my faith?
- Am I experiencing Christ's rest daily, or am I striving in my own strength?

Closing Prayer

Lord Jesus, thank You for being my true rest. Forgive me for striving in my own strength or neglecting fellowship with Your people. Teach me to rest in Your finished work, to walk in the Spirit, and to honor You with the first of my time and devotion. May my life be marked by peace in You and fruitfulness for Your glory. In Jesus' name, Amen.

Chapter 16

Fear – The Silent Thief of Faith
(2 Timothy 1:7)

"For God hath not given us the spirit of fear; but of power, and of love, and of a sound mind." (2 Timothy 1:7)

Introduction

Fear is one of the enemy's most subtle but deadly weapons. It does not shout like anger or boast like pride; instead, it creeps in quietly and weakens the believer's faith. Fear is the silent thief of courage, vision, and obedience.

The Bible repeats "fear not" 365 times — one for each day of the year. This is no coincidence. God knew that fear would be a daily challenge for His children, so He gave a daily reminder: "Do not fear, for I am with you" (Isaiah 41:10).

Fear and faith cannot dwell together. One always pushes the other out. When fear rises, faith sinks; when faith rises, fear flees.

What Is Fear?

Fear is more than an emotion — it is a spirit. Fear is a natural human reaction to danger, but it becomes destructive when it controls our decisions. Fear magnifies threats and blinds us to God's promises. Someone once described fear as False Evidence Appearing Real. Most of the things we worry about never actually happen, yet fear robs us of peace and courage.

Fear is like a prison guard that locks people inside cages of inaction, regret, and doubt.

Fear in the Bible

The Bible is filled with examples of how fear crippled people's faith:
- The Israelites at the Red Sea (Exodus 14:10–12): Instead of remembering God's power over Egypt, they cried in fear,

ready to go back to slavery.
- The ten spies (Numbers 13:31–33): They exaggerated the giants and saw themselves as grasshoppers, though God had promised victory.
- King Saul (1 Samuel 17:11): Though a giant himself, he trembled before Goliath, proving that fear reduces even the mighty.
- Job (Job 3:25–26): Job admitted, "The thing which I greatly feared is come upon me." His constant dread opened a door for the enemy.

But there are also stories where people conquered fear through faith:
- David faced Goliath with courage born from trust in God (1 Samuel 17:45).
- Joshua heard God's voice saying, "Be strong and courageous; do not be afraid, for the Lord your God is with you" (Joshua 1:9).
- Mary was told by the angel, "Fear not, for you have found favour with God" (Luke 1:30).

The Destructive Power of Fear

Fear does not stay silent; it bears bitter fruit:
- It distorts reality: The spies saw giants but forgot God's power.
- It paralyzes obedience: Many delay stepping into God's calling because of fear of failure.

- It enslaves the mind: Fear causes worry, anxiety, depression, and sleepless nights.
- It affects health: Doctors confirm that chronic fear can cause high blood pressure, heart disease, and mental breakdown.
- It opens the door to sin: Abraham lied about Sarah (Genesis 12:13) and Peter denied Jesus (Luke 22:57) — both out of fear.

Fear is not harmless. It is a thief that steals joy, health, faith, and destiny.

The Fear of the Lord vs. the Spirit of Fear

The Bible makes a vital distinction:
- The spirit of fear enslaves, confuses, and destroys. It is from the devil.
- The fear of the Lord is holy reverence for God. It is the beginning of wisdom (Proverbs 9:10), a fountain of life (Proverbs 14:27), and a strong confidence (Proverbs 14:26).

The spirit of fear destroys, but the fear of the Lord builds.

Why Do People Fear?

- Fear of the unknown: Many hesitate to take steps of faith because they cannot see the full outcome.
- Fear of rejection: Some stay silent about their faith or compromise truth to be accepted.

- Fear of failure: Others never pursue God's calling because they are afraid they might fall.
- Fear of loss: Job feared losing his children and wealth, and eventually experienced what he dreaded.

Every fear has one root — a lack of trust in God's character.

Overcoming Fear with Faith

God has already given us weapons against fear:
1. God's Presence – "Fear not, for I am with you" (Isaiah 41:10). When God is with us, nothing can overcome us.
2. God's Promises – Faith is built by hearing the Word (Romans 10:17). Meditating on His promises drives out fear.
3. God's Love – "Perfect love casts out fear" (1 John 4:18). Knowing God loves us removes fear of rejection or failure.
4. Prayer and Surrender – Cast all your cares upon Him (1 Peter 5:7). Fear thrives where worries are kept, but dies where they are surrendered.
5. Action in Faith – Courage is not the absence of fear, but moving forward despite it. Like Peter stepping out of the boat (Matthew 14:29).

Interactive Q&A

Q1: What is fear according to the Bible?
A1: Fear is a spirit not given by God (2 Timothy 1:7). It is an inner dread that magnifies problems, weakens faith, and enslaves the heart.

Q2: How did fear affect people in Scripture?
A2: It made Israel doubt at the Red Sea, caused the spies to see themselves as grasshoppers, paralyzed King Saul, and troubled Job. Fear led to disobedience, confusion, and loss.

Q3: Why is fear dangerous to a believer?
A3: Fear paralyzes action, distorts reality, damages health, and opens doors to sin and the enemy's attacks.

Q4: How is the fear of the Lord different from the spirit of fear?
A4: The spirit of fear enslaves and destroys, but the fear of the Lord is reverence, leading to wisdom, confidence, and life.

Q5: How can Christians overcome fear?
A5: By trusting God's presence, standing on His promises, praying and surrendering worries, living in His love, and acting in faith even when afraid.

Reflection Points

- What fears have silently controlled my decisions?
- Have I allowed fear of failure, rejection, or loss to hinder my obedience?

- Am I living in the tormenting spirit of fear or the liberating fear of the Lord?
- What Scripture promises can I hold onto when fear strikes?
- What one step of courage is God asking me to take today?

Closing Prayer

Heavenly Father, I thank You that You have not given me the spirit of fear, but of power, love, and a sound mind. Forgive me for the times I allowed fear to control my choices. Today I renounce fear and embrace faith. Fill me with Your Spirit, surround me with Your perfect love, and remind me daily of Your presence. Strengthen me to take bold steps of obedience, trusting You in every situation. I choose to walk by faith and not by fear. In Jesus' name, Amen.

Chapter 17

From Gift to Skill – Excelling in Your God-Given Calling
(Proverbs 22:29; Exodus 31:1–11)

"Seest thou a man diligent in his business? he shall stand before kings; he shall not stand before mean men." (Proverbs 22:29)

Introduction

A gift is the seed; skill is the harvest. Many people are gifted, but not all are skilful. The Bible shows us that gifts are not enough — they must be sharpened, trained, and refined until they shine with excellence. A raw gift is like an uncut diamond — valuable, but not yet beautiful or useful.

Proverbs 22:29 reminds us that diligence and refinement elevate a person. A man may be gifted, but it is skill, consistency, and discipline that bring him before kings. Bezaleel was not only called by God, but also filled with wisdom, knowledge, and skill to carry out God's assignment (Exodus 31:2–5). This shows us that it is not enough to have a gift — it must be diligently developed until it brings glory to God and blessing to the body of Christ.

The Call of Every Believer

Every Christian is called to service, not just pastors or preachers. God calls us all with a holy calling (2 Timothy 1:9). Just as every part of the body has its unique role, each believer is essential to the health of the body of Christ (Romans 12:5). No calling is insignificant — the eye cannot replace the hand, and the ear cannot replace the mouth.

When one member fails to function, the whole body suffers. This truth reminds us that discovering and embracing our calling is both a personal duty and a kingdom responsibility.

The Danger of Misplaced Function

A duck swims gracefully in water but looks clumsy on land. Likewise, people become ineffective when they step outside their God-given function. Envying another's calling or trying to imitate them only brings frustration and confusion.

Moses was called to lead; Bezaleel was called to craftsmanship. If Bezaleel tried to lead Israel, or Moses tried to build the tabernacle, both would have failed. Similarly, if we insist on walking in someone else's calling, we end up wasting time and weakening the body of Christ.

From Gift to Skill

A gift is potential, but skill is developed excellence. Bezaleel was gifted, but he also became skilful, devising cunning works with gold, silver, stones, and wood (Exodus 31:3–5).

- Gift is the raw material.
- Skill is the refined product.

Without training, discipline, and practice, a gift remains raw and underdeveloped. Skill requires:
- Prayer for God's wisdom.
- Study to gain knowledge.
- Practice to sharpen ability.
- Diligence to remain consistent.

A singer who refuses to train their voice or a preacher who never studies the Word may still have a gift, but without skill, their ministry will not edify the church.

Even in Babylon, Daniel and his friends were chosen not only because they were gifted, but also because they were "skilful in all wisdom, and cunning in knowledge" (Daniel 1:4). Their gifts were refined into excellence, which qualified them to stand before kings. In the same way, our gifts must be trained, sharpened, and disciplined if we are to be effective in God's kingdom.

The Cost of Neglecting Skill

Neglecting to sharpen your gift not only limits you, but it also damages the body of Christ. A dull axe wastes time and energy (Ecclesiastes 10:10). A lazy hunter who refuses to cook what he catches goes hungry (Proverbs 12:27).

Likewise, a believer who refuses to refine their calling weakens the effectiveness of the church. Poor preparation, lack of training, or laziness makes ministry clumsy and sometimes harmful. A gift that is not sharpened into skill may even bring shame instead of glory to God.

Wisdom for Excellence

Excellence is not optional in the kingdom — it honours God and builds His church. We are called to serve with our best, not with mediocrity.

Keys to excellence:
- Be wise-hearted: God imparts wisdom to those with willing hearts (Exodus 31:6).
- Be diligent: Keep training, practicing, and improving your gift.
- Be humble: Accept your place with joy instead of envying others.
- Be Spirit-filled: The Spirit gives life to our skill, preventing pride and empowering effectiveness.

Excellence is the balance of Spirit and skill. One without the other is incomplete.

Interactive Q&A

Q1: What do you understand by calling?
A1: A calling is God's personal assignment for each believer within the body of Christ, given according to His purpose and grace (2 Timothy 1:9).

Q2: Do you believe all Christians are called by God? If yes, what is your calling? If no, why not?
A2: Yes, all believers are called with a holy calling (2 Timothy 1:9). Each person has a unique role in the body of Christ

(Romans 12:5). The challenge is to discover, accept, and faithfully serve in it.

Q3: What must come before calling?
A3: Salvation comes first. God saves us, then calls us to serve Him with our gifts (2 Timothy 1:9). Without salvation, a calling cannot be fulfilled in God's way.

Q4: What should we do after knowing our calling, and why?
A4: We must refine our gift into skill through prayer, study, practice, and diligence so that we can serve with excellence and not weaken the body of Christ (2 Timothy 2:15).

Q5: Is it right to function in another person's calling? Why or why not?
A5: No. Every believer has a unique role. Trying to function in someone else's place brings confusion and damages the body, just as the eye cannot do the work of the mouth (Romans 12:4–6).

Reflection Points

- Am I functioning in my God-given calling, or am I trying to copy someone else?
- Have I left my gift raw, or am I refining it into skill through diligence and training?
- Is the body of Christ suffering because of my neglect or mediocrity?
- Do I value my unique calling as essential to God's plan?
- How can I sharpen my skill this week in service to God?

Closing Prayer

Heavenly Father, thank You for calling me into Your service. Forgive me for times I left my gift undeveloped or envied another's calling. Teach me to embrace my place in the body of Christ with humility and joy. Help me to refine my gift into skill through diligence, training, and the wisdom of Your Spirit. May my service bring honour to You and strength to Your church. In Jesus' name, Amen.

Chapter 18

Power – The Evidence of the Kingdom

(Matthew 10:1)

"And when he had called unto him his twelve disciples, he gave them power against unclean spirits, to cast them out, and to heal all manner of sickness and all manner of disease." (Matthew 10:1)

Introduction

Power is inseparable from Christianity. To remove power from Christianity is to strip it of its essence. As Paul declared: "The kingdom of God is not in word, but in power"

(1 Corinthians 4:20). Christianity is the living demonstration of God's power at work in the believer's life (Romans 1:16).

But while power is a mark of true Christianity, power is not the whole of Christianity. Just as walking is natural to humans but not their entire purpose, so power is normal to Christians but not the ultimate focus. Christianity is a life of faith, holiness, love, and obedience — power simply complements this life, never replacing it.

Christianity Is Power — But Power Is Not Christianity

It is crucial to know the difference. God is love (1 John 4:16), yet love is not God. Likewise, Christianity is power, yet power is not Christianity. This distinction protects us from deception, especially in a world where power demonstrations are often turned into shows.

Power in Christianity is not for entertainment but for edification. Paul reminded the Corinthians that his preaching was "not with enticing words of man's wisdom, but in demonstration of the Spirit and of power: That your faith should not stand in the wisdom of men, but in the power of God" (1 Corinthians 2:4–5). The purpose of power is not to impress but to root faith in God alone, not in the charisma of men.

Power Is Given to All Believers

Matthew 10:1 shows us that Jesus gave His disciples power over demons, sickness, and disease. This was not limited to "special apostles" — every believer in Christ has access to this same power.

- "Them that believe" (Mark 16:17–18) are promised signs, deliverance, and healing authority.
- Faith the size of a mustard seed can move mountains (Matthew 17:20).
- The Holy Spirit empowers all Christians, not just pastors, prophets, or "anointed men of God" (Acts 1:8).

If you are saved, you are called. If you are called, you are empowered.

The Danger of Running After Power

Today, many believers run from one prophet to another, from crusade to crusade, searching for miracles. This is not faith — it is restlessness and immaturity. True faith waits upon the Lord (Isaiah 40:31).

Running after power leads to deception. Pharaoh's magicians imitated Moses' miracle (Exodus 7). Not every display of power is from God.
- Running after power weakens trust. Instead of looking to Christ, such believers look to personalities.
- Running after power exposes you to danger. Strange miracles

often come with hidden sorrows (Proverbs 10:22).

The solution is to stand firm in your faith, trust God's Word, and know that His power already resides in you.

Miracles vs. Magic

Not all that glitters is gold. Not every supernatural act is a miracle.

- Miracles are divine works of God, rooted in His truth, and leading to life.
- Magic is deception from Satan, designed to enslave and destroy (1 Peter 5:8).

Miracles come with peace and blessing. Magic comes with bondage and sorrow. Miracles glorify God; magic glorifies man and leads astray.

Waiting for God's Appointed Time

Faith knows how to wait. God's power works in His timing, not ours. "For the vision is yet for an appointed time… though it tarry, wait for it; because it will surely come, it will not tarry" (Habakkuk 2:3).

While false powers promise instant results, God's miracles arrive with perfection and no sorrow attached. The blessing of the Lord makes rich and adds no sorrow with it (Proverbs 10:22).

Interactive Q&A

Q1: Is power Christianity? Justify your answer.
A1: Christianity is power, but power is not Christianity. Power complements faith, holiness, and love, but should never replace them (1 Corinthians 4:20).

Q2: Is power given to all believers or only men of God?
A2: Power is given to all believers. Jesus said, "These signs shall follow them that believe" (Mark 16:17–18). Every Christian has authority through Christ.

Q3: Is it right for a believer to run after power? What should they do instead?
A3: No. Running after power is a sign of weak faith and opens doors to deception. Instead, believers should trust God's Word, wait upon Him, and exercise the power He has already given them (Isaiah 40:31).

Q4: What is the difference between miracle and magic?
A4: Miracles are divine acts of God that glorify Him and bring blessing without sorrow. Magic is counterfeit power from Satan, designed to deceive and destroy (Exodus 7; Proverbs 10:22).

Q5: Why is God's timing important when we seek His power?
A5: Because God's miracles come at the appointed time and

bring peace without sorrow (Habakkuk 2:3; Proverbs 10:22). Rushing ahead often leads to deception or disappointment.

Reflection Points

- Am I seeking Christ Himself, or just His power?
- Do I believe that God has already given me authority as a believer?
- Am I running after prophets, or am I standing on God's Word in faith?
- Do I know how to discern between miracles and magic?
- Am I willing to wait for God's timing instead of forcing a shortcut?

Closing Prayer

Heavenly Father, thank You for the gift of Your power through Jesus Christ. Forgive me for times I doubted and chased after human displays instead of trusting You. Teach me to walk in faith, exercising the authority You have already given me. Help me to discern between true miracles and false signs, and to wait patiently for Your perfect timing. Let my life glorify You, not through empty show, but through the genuine power of the Holy Spirit at work in me. In Jesus' name, Amen.

Chapter 19

Fasting – The Hidden Strength of the Believer

(Matthew 6:16–18)

"But thou, when thou fastest, anoint thine head, and wash thy face; That thou appear not unto men to fast, but unto thy Father which is in secret: and thy Father, which seeth in secret, shall reward thee openly."
(Matthew 6:17–18)

Introduction

Fasting is one of the most overlooked spiritual disciplines in the Christian life. In Matthew 6, Jesus spoke of "when you fast", not "if you fast". That single word when shows that fasting is not optional but expected of every believer.

Fasting is not merely going without food; it is setting aside the desires of the flesh in order to seek God with greater intensity. Without prayer, fasting loses its meaning and becomes nothing more than a hunger strike. But when joined with prayer, it becomes a powerful key to spiritual breakthrough.

What Fasting Really Means

At its core, fasting is self-denial for spiritual gain. It is the act of saying "no" to physical appetite so you can say "yes" more deeply to God.

- It is surrender — showing God that His presence matters more than food.
- It is humility — bowing before Him in weakness and dependence.
- It is warfare — a weapon that weakens the flesh but strengthens the spirit.

Paul captured it when he said, "I discipline my body and bring it into subjection" (1 Corinthians 9:27).

Biblical Models of Fasting

The Bible gives many examples of fasting:

- Moses fasted forty days as he received God's law (Exodus 34:28).
- Daniel fasted for understanding and breakthrough (Daniel 10:2–3).
- Esther and the Jews fasted for deliverance (Esther 4:16).
- Jesus fasted forty days before launching His ministry (Matthew 4:1–2).
- The early church fasted before sending out missionaries (Acts 13:2–3).

Each fast carried a specific purpose — revelation, protection, empowerment, or consecration.

Types of Fasting

Though the Bible does not prescribe rigid formulas, several patterns emerge:

- Private Fasting – Between you and God (Matthew 6:16).
- Corporate Fasting – Families, churches, or nations humbling themselves together (Joel 2:15–16).
- Dry Fasting – Complete abstinence from food and water for a period (Esther 4:16).
- Partial Fasting – Restricting certain foods, like Daniel's fast (Daniel 10:2–3).

The length and form may vary, but the heart of fasting remains the same: seeking God above all else.

Why Believers Must Fast

Fasting is not just tradition — it carries divine purpose:

1. Obedience to Christ – Jesus expects His disciples to fast (Matthew 6:16).
2. Spiritual Power – Some victories come only through fasting and prayer (Mark 9:29).
3. Breaking Yokes – Fasting is God's chosen weapon to loose bands of wickedness (Isaiah 58:6).
4. Humility – David humbled his soul with fasting (Psalm 35:13).
5. Repentance – The people of Nineveh fasted and God spared them (Jonah 3:5–10).
6. Consecration – Daniel sought God with fasting and prayer (Daniel 9:3).
7. Worship – Anna served God with fasting and prayer continually (Luke 2:37).
8. Discipline – Fasting trains us to master our appetites instead of being mastered by them.

Fasting With the Right Attitude

Jesus warned against hypocrisy in fasting. The Pharisees disfigured their faces to appear spiritual, but God rejected their show (Matthew 6:16). True fasting is not to impress people but to please God.

- Keep it private.
- Combine it with prayer, worship, and scripture.
- Let it lead to transformation, not pride.

The Father who sees in secret promises to reward openly.

Practical Benefits of Fasting

When done in faith, fasting impacts every part of life:

- Spiritually – greater sensitivity to God's voice, spiritual breakthroughs, deliverance.
- Emotionally – humility, clarity, peace.
- Physically – cleansing and discipline for the body when practiced wisely.

David testified, "My knees are weak through fasting" (Psalm 109:24). The flesh may weaken, but the spirit is renewed with strength.

Interactive Q&A

Q1: What is fasting in the Christian sense?
A1: Fasting is abstaining from food or other pleasures for spiritual purposes, to humble the flesh and seek God more intensely (1 Corinthians 9:27).

Q2: Who are some biblical examples of fasting?
A2: Moses, Daniel, Esther, Jesus, and the early church all practiced fasting for revelation, deliverance, empowerment, and consecration.

Q3: What are the main types of fasting?
A3: Private, corporate, dry, and partial fasting. Each serves the same purpose: to draw closer to God (Daniel 10:2–3; Joel 2:15–16).

Q4: Why should Christians fast?
A4: For obedience to Christ, spiritual power, breaking yokes, humility, repentance, consecration, worship, and discipline (Isaiah 58:6; Mark 9:29).

Q5: What makes fasting acceptable to God?
A5: Fasting must be joined with prayer, sincerity, humility, and obedience. Without prayer, fasting is just a hunger strike.

Reflection Points

- Do I treat fasting as a duty or as a privilege?
- Am I fasting to impress others, or to seek God sincerely?
- What spiritual battles in my life might require fasting?

- Do I combine fasting with prayer and the Word?
- Am I willing to discipline my flesh to strengthen my spirit?

Closing Prayer

Father, thank You for teaching me the power of fasting. Help me to approach it not as a burden but as a blessing, not to impress men but to honour You. Break every yoke in my life, sharpen my spiritual sensitivity, and help me to walk in victory. Teach me to fast with humility, prayer, and faith, that my life may bring You glory. In Jesus' name, Amen.

Chapter 20

Prayer – The Strongest Weapon of the Believer
(1 Thessalonians 5:17)

"Pray without ceasing." (1 Thessalonians 5:17)

Introduction

Prayer is the lifeline of the Christian faith. Just as breathing sustains the body, prayer sustains the spirit. Without prayer, a believer is powerless, vulnerable, and easily defeated. With prayer, a believer is strengthened, protected, and equipped to overcome.

The command to "pray without ceasing" (1 Thessalonians 5:17) does not mean spending every second on your knees, but cultivating a life of constant communion with God. Whether in joy or in sorrow, in strength or in weakness, in public or in private — prayer must be the Christian's unbroken habit.

What Prayer Really Is

Prayer is more than reciting words. It is communion with God — speaking to Him, listening to Him, and aligning with His will.

- Prayer is relationship — drawing near to God as Father (Matthew 6:9).
- Prayer is warfare — wielding spiritual authority against the powers of darkness (Ephesians 6:18).
- Prayer is surrender — leaving the battle in God's hands (2 Chronicles 20:15).
- Prayer is power — opening the door for God to act in situations (James 5:16).

A Christian who prays is a Christian who lives in the strength of God.

Why Prayer Is Non-Negotiable

Jesus warned against lukewarm Christianity (Revelation 3:15–16). Prayer is one of the four pillars that keep the believer spiritually hot: prayer, holiness, the Word, and evangelism. Neglecting prayer weakens all the rest.

- A prayerless Christian is a powerless Christian.
- A prayerful Christian is a powerful Christian.

Prayer is not optional — it is the very atmosphere in which a Christian survives.

The Power of Persistent Prayer

Persistence is the secret of answered prayer. Jesus told the parable of the persistent widow who obtained justice because she refused to give up (Luke 18:1–8).

- Every prayer counts — like drops of water that wear down a stone.
- Breakthrough may take time — Hannah prayed for years before God gave her Samuel (1 Samuel 1:9–20).
- Delays are not denials — Daniel's prayer was answered from the first day, though the angel was delayed by opposition (Daniel 10:12–13).

Never stop praying. Your next prayer could be the key that opens the door.

When Prayer Must Be Combined With Fasting

Some spiritual battles require more than prayer alone. Jesus said, "This kind goeth not out but by prayer and fasting" (Matthew 17:21).

- Esther and the Jews fasted and prayed before their deliverance (Esther 4:15–17).
- Nehemiah fasted and prayed before rebuilding Jerusalem (Nehemiah 1:4).
- The church at Antioch fasted and prayed before sending missionaries (Acts 13:2–3).

Fasting sharpens prayer, humbles the flesh, and releases spiritual power.

The Consequences of Prayerlessness

The absence of prayer is deadly.

- John the Baptist was beheaded; no prayer was raised for him (Matthew 14:10).
- Stephen was stoned; the church mourned but did not intercede (Acts 7:59–60).
- But when Peter was imprisoned, the church prayed fervently — and God sent an angel to set him free (Acts 12:5–11).

- Paul and Silas prayed and sang hymns in prison, and the prison doors opened (Acts 16:25–26).

Where prayer is absent, defeat is near. Where prayer is present, miracles are inevitable.

A Life of Continuous Prayer

Prayer is not reserved for emergencies — it is to be the believer's lifestyle. Paul wrote: "Praying always with all prayer and supplication in the Spirit" (Ephesians 6:18).

- Pray in good times and bad.
- Pray for yourself and for others.
- Pray until the answer comes.
- Pray until peace fills your heart.

Prayer connects us to God's purpose and ensures His power flows through our lives.

Interactive Q&A

Q1: How often should Christians pray?
A1: Always. Scripture commands us to "pray without ceasing" (1 Thessalonians 5:17). Prayer must be continual and consistent.

Q2: What should a believer do when weary, troubled, or frustrated?
A2: Pray, not complain. Prayer brings peace, direction, and breakthrough (Luke 18:1; Philippians 4:6–7).

Q3: Why is prayer so important?
A3: Prayer brings power, strengthens faith, breaks yokes, opens doors, and keeps the believer spiritually hot (Acts 12:5; James 5:16).

Q4: What keeps a Christian spiritually hot, and what makes them cold?
A4: Prayer, holiness, the Word, and evangelism keep a believer hot. Neglecting these leads to lukewarmness (Revelation 3:15–16).

Q5: What happens when believers neglect prayer?
A5: They become powerless and vulnerable. Without prayer, John was beheaded and Stephen was stoned, but with prayer, Peter was delivered, and Paul and Silas were set free (Acts 12:5; Acts 16:25–26).

Reflection Points

- Do I treat prayer as a daily necessity or only as a last resort?
- Am I persistent in prayer, or do I give up too quickly?
- Do I combine prayer with fasting when necessary?
- Is my prayer life keeping me spiritually hot, or am I growing lukewarm?
- Who can I intercede for today?

Closing Prayer

Father, thank You for the gift of prayer. Forgive me for the times I neglected this weapon. Teach me to pray without ceasing, to persist in faith, and to never give up. Let my prayers shake mountains, bring deliverance, and glorify Your name. Make me a believer who is always hot in spirit through prayer, holiness, Your Word, and evangelism. In Jesus' name, Amen.

Chapter 21

Healing – The Children's Bread
(Matthew 8:16–17)

"When the even was come, they brought unto him many that were possessed with devils: and he cast out the spirits with his word, and healed all that were sick: That it might be fulfilled which was spoken by Esaias the prophet, saying, Himself took our infirmities, and bare our sicknesses."
(Matthew 8:16–17)

Introduction

Healing is not an optional benefit of the gospel — it is part of the foundation of salvation. Jesus did not only preach forgiveness; He demonstrated God's love through healing, deliverance, and restoration. Scripture declares: "God anointed Jesus of Nazareth with the Holy Ghost and with power, who went about doing good, and healing all that were oppressed of the devil" (Acts 10:38).

The same Jesus who healed the sick two thousand years ago is alive and unchanging today (Hebrews 13:8). Healing is not just something God can do; it is something He has already provided through Christ.

Healing Is a Finished Work

Isaiah spoke prophetically of the suffering of Christ: "But he was wounded for our transgressions, he was bruised for our iniquities: the chastisement of our peace was upon him; and with his stripes we are healed" (Isaiah 53:5). Notice the phrase: "we are healed." Not will be, not may be — we are healed. At the cross, Jesus bore both sin and sickness. Just as forgiveness is past tense — already paid for — so healing is past tense. Peter confirms this truth: "By whose stripes ye were healed" (1 Peter 2:24). If we were healed, then in God's eyes, healing is already done. Our role is to receive it by faith.

God's Will to Heal Everyone

Jesus never turned away a single person who came to Him in faith. Scripture repeatedly says, "He healed them all" (Matthew 12:15; Luke 6:19). Healing is the children's bread

(Matthew 15:26). If forgiveness of sins is available to all, then healing is also available to all, because both were purchased by the same sacrifice. Psalm 103:3 declares: "Who forgiveth all thine iniquities; who healeth all thy diseases."

We Are Called to Be the Healers

Jesus gave His disciples authority not only to receive healing but to administer it. He said: "They shall lay hands on the sick, and they shall recover" (Mark 16:18). Notice carefully — He did not say believers should remain the sick needing healing; He said believers should be the ones laying hands on the sick. This means we are not meant to live as the sick but as the healers, carrying the life of Christ to others. Every believer is a vessel of God's healing power. If you believe, you are not just waiting for a miracle — you are an agent of miracles.

The Means of Healing

God heals in many ways, but the source is always Christ:

1. Through Prayer – "The prayer of faith shall save the sick" (James 5:15).
2. Through the Word – "He sent His word, and healed them" (Psalm 107:20).

3. Through Laying on of Hands – Believers will lay hands on the sick and they shall recover (Mark 16:18).
4. Through Communion – The body and blood of Christ are a channel of healing (1 Corinthians 11:23–24).
5. Through Faith – Jesus often said, "Thy faith hath made thee whole" (Mark 5:34).

Hindrances to Healing

God's power is unlimited, but unbelief can block its manifestation:

- Unbelief (Mark 6:5–6).
- Unforgiveness (Mark 11:25).
- Willful sin (John 5:14).
- Lack of persistence in prayer.

Faith is not hoping God will do it; it is standing on what God has already done.

Healing and Wholeness

Healing is more than the removal of pain; it is the restoration of complete wholeness — spirit, soul, and body (1 Thessalonians 5:23). Ten lepers were healed, but only one returned to thank Jesus — and he was made whole (Luke 17:19). Wholeness means living beyond healing, walking in divine health, gratitude, and obedience. God's desire is not just to heal us once, but to keep us healthy daily as we abide in Him.

Interactive Q&A

Q1: Is healing God's will for everyone?
A1: Yes. Jesus healed all who came to Him in faith, and Scripture shows forgiveness and healing are both included in redemption (Psalm 103:3; Matthew 12:15).

Q2: What does Isaiah 53:5 teach about healing?
A2: It shows that healing is already accomplished in the past tense. 'By His stripes we are healed.' It is a finished work of the cross, just like forgiveness of sins.

Q3: What does Mark 16:18 reveal about believers?
A3: Believers are called to be the healers, not the sick. We are empowered to lay hands on the sick and see them recover, carrying God's power to others.

Q4: What are some hindrances to receiving healing?
A4: Unbelief, unforgiveness, willful sin, and lack of persistence in prayer (Mark 6:5–6; John 5:14).

Q5: What is the difference between healing and wholeness?
A5: Healing removes sickness, but wholeness restores spirit, soul, and body — enabling believers to live in lasting health and peace (Luke 17:19).

Reflection Points

- Do I believe healing is already mine because of the finished work of Christ?
- Am I living as the sick needing healing, or as the healer carrying Christ's power?
- Do I align my faith with God's Word or with my feelings and symptoms?
- Are there hindrances (unbelief, unforgiveness, sin) blocking healing in my life?
- Am I seeking not just healing, but wholeness in every area of life?

Closing Prayer

Father, thank You that healing is already finished through the stripes of Jesus. I believe Your Word — that I was healed at the cross. I reject sickness as part of my identity and embrace divine health in Christ. Make me not only a receiver of healing but a carrier of Your healing power to others. Help me to walk daily in wholeness of spirit, soul, and body. In Jesus' mighty name, Amen.

Chapter 22

Water Baptism – Buried with Christ, Raised to New Life

(Romans 6:3–4)

"Know ye not, that so many of us as were baptized into Jesus Christ were baptized into his death? Therefore we are buried with him by baptism into death: that like as Christ was raised up from the dead by the glory of the Father, even so we also should walk in newness of life." (Romans 6:3–4)

Introduction

Water baptism is one of the most visible and powerful ordinances given by JESUS CHRIST. It is not merely a tradition or formality; it is a command and a testimony. JESUS said: "Go ye therefore, and teach all nations, baptizing them in the name of the Father, and of the Son, and of the Holy Ghost" (Matthew 28:19).

From the day of Pentecost onward, those who believed were baptized as the public mark of their repentance and new life in CHRIST (Acts 2:38, 41). To understand baptism rightly, we must return to the meaning of the word itself, the New Testament practice, and the questions often debated today.

The Meaning of Baptism

The word baptism comes from the Greek verb baptizō (βαπτίζω), which means: "to immerse, dip, or submerge in water." It was used in ancient Greek to describe cloth being dipped in dye or a ship sinking beneath the waves.

This meaning shows that baptism is not sprinkling a few drops of water, but a full immersion — a complete identification with CHRIST in death, burial, and resurrection. Paul explains: "Buried with him in baptism, wherein also ye are risen with him through the faith of the operation of God" (Colossians 2:12). Burial is not partial — it is complete. Baptism by immersion most fully represents this truth.

Baptism: A Command and a Witness

- A command of CHRIST: JESUS linked discipleship with baptism (Matthew 28:19–20).
- A confession of faith: Baptism is the believer's public declaration: "I belong to JESUS."
- A covenant sign: It marks the believer's break with the old life and entrance into the new (Romans 6:4).

It is not the water itself that saves but the faith and repentance behind it. As Peter wrote: "Not the putting away of the filth of the flesh, but the answer of a good conscience toward God" (1 Peter 3:21).

Infant Baptism or Believer's Baptism?

This is a common question in the church today.

- Infant Baptism: Practiced in some traditions, often as a cultural or covenant sign. Infants are dedicated, but they cannot yet personally repent or believe.
- Believer's Baptism (Adult or Youth): The consistent New Testament pattern is faith first, then baptism:
  * "They that gladly received his word were baptized" (Acts 2:41).
  * "But when they believed Philip preaching the things concerning the kingdom of God… they were baptized, both men and women" (Acts 8:12).

* The Ethiopian eunuch confessed faith before baptism (Acts 8:36–37).

Faith and repentance are always prerequisites. An infant cannot repent, confess, or believe. Therefore, baptism is rightly administered to those who are old enough to respond to the gospel in faith.

Infants may be dedicated to the LORD, just as Samuel was (1 Samuel 1:27–28), and JESUS blessed little children (Mark 10:14). But baptism is for those who can personally believe and declare JESUS as LORD.

Why Immersion?

Because baptism means "to immerse," the New Testament examples are clear:
- John baptized where there was "much water" (John 3:23).
- Philip and the Ethiopian eunuch "went down both into the water… and came up out of the water" (Acts 8:38–39).
- Baptism is a burial (Romans 6:4) — best pictured by full immersion.

In Whose Name? — Matthew 28:19 and Acts 2:38

- JESUS commanded baptism "in the name of the Father, and of the Son, and of the Holy Ghost" (Matthew

28:19).

- The apostles baptized "in the name of Jesus Christ" (Acts 2:38; 10:48; 19:5), emphasizing Christ's authority and identity as the crucified and risen Lord.

These are not competing formulas. Baptizing in the Triune Name honors the command of JESUS, and doing so in/into the name of Jesus declares the Person and work by which salvation came. Many churches rightly articulate both realities in one service.

Who Should Be Baptized?

The New Testament pattern is believers' baptism — those who repent and believe (Acts 2:41; 8:12).

Infants are precious to God (Mark 10:14), but baptism follows personal faith. Families may dedicate children to the LORD, then lead them toward repentance and faith that issues in baptism when they can personally confess CHRIST.

Water and the Spirit

JESUS spoke of being "born of water and of the Spirit" (John 3:5). The New Testament shows distinct yet related graces:

- New birth by the Spirit through faith in CHRIST (John 1:12–

13; Titus 3:5).
- Water baptism, the sign and seal of repentance and faith (Acts 2:38).
- Empowerment by the HOLY GHOST for witness and holy living (Acts 1:8; 8:14–17; 10:44–48; 19:1–6).

Baptism doesn't replace the Spirit's work; it confesses and cooperates with it.

Preparing for Baptism

1. Repent: Turn from sin to GOD (Acts 3:19).
2. Believe: Trust JESUS CHRIST alone for salvation (Romans 10:9–10).
3. Renounce: Break with old allegiances and hidden works of darkness (2 Corinthians 6:14–18).
4. Confess: Publicly declare faith in CHRIST before witnesses (Matthew 10:32).
5. Join: Commit to a local church for teaching, fellowship, and mission (Acts 2:42–47).

After Baptism: Walking in Newness of Life

Baptism is a beginning, not an ending:

- Daily holiness: "Reckon" yourself dead to sin, alive to GOD (Romans 6:11–14).

- Word & Prayer: Abide in CHRIST (John 15:4–7; Acts 2:42).
- Witness: Live boldly and share the gospel (Matthew 5:16; Acts 1:8).
- Endurance: Expect temptation after your public stand (Matthew 3:16–4:1); resist steadfastly (1 Peter 5:8–10).

Re-Baptism?

Acts 19:1–6 shows disciples baptized into John's baptism were baptized again into Jesus when they heard the full gospel. Re-baptism may be fitting when:
- The first event preceded genuine repentance and faith, or
- It was not Christian baptism (e.g., purely cultural/ritual).

We should not be casual with re-baptism, but neither should we leave consciences clouded when Scripture's pattern calls for clarity.

Interactive Q&A

Q1: What does the word "baptism" mean in Greek?
A1: Baptizō means to immerse, dip, or submerge. This shows that baptism is not sprinkling but immersion, picturing burial and resurrection with CHRIST.

Q2: Is baptism optional for believers?
A2: No. JESUS commanded baptism for all who believe

(Matthew 28:19). It does not save by itself, but obedience to CHRIST requires it.

Q3: Should infants be baptized?
A3: The New Testament shows only believers being baptized after repentance and faith. Infants may be dedicated, but baptism is for those who personally believe (Acts 2:41; Acts 8:12).

Q4: Why is immersion important?
A4: Immersion best pictures burial and resurrection with CHRIST (Romans 6:4; Colossians 2:12). Sprinkling does not fully display this truth.

Q5: What happens after baptism?
A5: You have publicly declared death to the old life and risen to new life in CHRIST. You must now walk in obedience, holiness, fellowship, and witness (Romans 6:11–14; Acts 2:42).

Reflection Points

- Have I been baptized since I personally believed in CHRIST?
- Do I understand baptism as identification with His death and resurrection?
- Am I living daily as one buried to sin and alive to GOD?
- Am I helping others prepare for baptism through teaching and discipleship?

- Do I treat baptism as a one-time ritual or as the beginning of a lifelong walk with CHRIST?

Closing Prayer

Lord JESUS, thank You for calling me to follow You in baptism. Thank You that I am buried with You and raised to walk in newness of life. Strengthen me to live out my baptism daily — dying to sin, living to GOD, and shining as Your witness. Keep me faithful in obedience until the day I see You face to face. In Your name I pray, Amen.

Chapter 23

Baptism of the Holy Spirit – Endued with Power from on High

(Acts 1:4–5, 8)

"And, being assembled together with them, commanded them that they should not depart from Jerusalem, but wait for the promise of the Father, which, saith he, ye have heard of me. For John truly baptized with water; but ye shall be baptized with the Holy Ghost not many days hence... But ye shall receive power, after that the Holy Ghost is come upon you: and ye shall be witnesses unto me both in Jerusalem, and in all Judaea, and in Samaria, and unto the uttermost part of the earth." (Acts 1:4–5, 8)

Introduction

The baptism of the Holy Spirit is not a doctrine invented by men; it is the promise of the Father, fulfilled through the Son, and ministered by the Spirit Himself. JESUS told His disciples not to attempt ministry until they were clothed with power from above (Luke 24:49). Salvation prepares us for heaven, but Holy Spirit baptism equips us for earth — to live victoriously and to minister effectively.

On the day of Pentecost, this promise became reality. The fearful disciples were transformed into bold witnesses when the Spirit came upon them (Acts 2:1–4). That same promise did not expire with the apostles. Peter declared: "For the promise is unto you, and to your children, and to all that are afar off, even as many as the Lord our God shall call" (Acts 2:39).

The Promise of the Father

Long before Pentecost, God had spoken through the prophets:
- Joel: "I will pour out my Spirit upon all flesh" (Joel 2:28–29).
- Ezekiel: "I will put my Spirit within you" (Ezekiel 36:27).
- Isaiah: "I will pour my Spirit upon thy seed" (Isaiah 44:3).

JESUS reaffirmed this promise: "Behold, I send the promise of my Father upon you" (Luke 24:49). The Father promised, the Son secured, and the Spirit delivered.

Distinction from Water Baptism

John the Baptist prepared the way for JESUS, saying: "I indeed baptize you with water unto repentance: but he that cometh after me... he shall baptize you with the Holy Ghost, and with fire" (Matthew 3:11).

- Water baptism symbolizes repentance and new life.
- Spirit baptism empowers for service and holy living.

At salvation, the Spirit dwells in you (John 14:17). At Spirit baptism, the Spirit comes upon you for power (Acts 1:8). Both are vital, but they are not the same.

The Day of Pentecost and Beyond

The baptism of the Spirit first manifested at Pentecost:
- The disciples were filled (Acts 2:4).
- Peter, once a coward, boldly preached (Acts 2:14–41).
- Three thousand souls were saved in one day.

But Pentecost was not a one-time event. The Spirit fell again in Samaria (Acts 8:14–17), in the household of Cornelius (Acts 10:44–46), and in Ephesus (Acts 19:1–6).

This shows the baptism of the Spirit is for every believer in every generation.

Why the Holy Spirit Baptism Is Needed

1. Power to Witness – Without the Spirit, evangelism is human effort. With the Spirit, it becomes God's demonstration (Acts 1:8).
2. Boldness to Speak – Spirit-filled believers pray and preach with fire (Acts 4:31).
3. Victory Over Sin – The Spirit enables mortification of the flesh (Romans 8:13).
4. Spiritual Gifts – Tongues, prophecy, healing, discernment — these come as the Spirit wills (1 Corinthians 12:7–11).
5. Deeper Intimacy with God – The Spirit helps us cry, "Abba, Father" (Romans 8:15–16).

The Evidence of Spirit Baptism

In the book of Acts, the initial physical evidence was speaking in tongues (Acts 2:4; Acts 10:44–46; Acts 19:6). Tongues are not the whole of Spirit baptism, but they are the consistent sign.

The ongoing evidence is a life transformed:
- Love and holiness (Galatians 5:22–23).

- Power in witness.
- Victory over fear.

Misconceptions About the Holy Spirit Baptism

- It is not automatic at salvation. Every believer has the Spirit, but not every believer is baptized in the Spirit (Acts 8:14–16).
- It is not reserved for pastors. The promise is for all believers (Acts 2:39).
- It is not emotional hype. True Spirit baptism results in lasting fruit, not fleeting feelings.
- It is not a one-time event. We must be continually filled (Ephesians 5:18).

How to Receive the Holy Spirit Baptism

1. Thirst – Hunger for more of God (Matthew 5:6; John 7:37).
2. Ask – The Spirit is God's gift to His children (Luke 11:13).
3. Believe – Receive by faith, not by striving (Galatians 3:2).
4. Yield – Surrender fully to God's will.
5. Receive – Open your mouth in prayer and let the Spirit give utterance (Acts 2:4).

Living the Spirit-Filled Life Daily

Spirit baptism is the doorway; Spirit-filled living is the journey.

- Continual Infilling: "Be filled with the Spirit" (Ephesians 5:18).
- Prayer in the Spirit: Building up your faith (Jude 20).
- Walking in the Spirit: Victory over the flesh (Galatians 5:16).
- Serving in the Spirit: Using gifts for God's glory (1 Corinthians 12:7).
- Witnessing in the Spirit: Preaching Christ boldly.

Interactive Q&A

Q1: What is the baptism of the Holy Spirit?
A1: It is an immersion into the Spirit, distinct from salvation, giving believers power, boldness, and gifts to live and witness effectively (Acts 1:8).

Q2: Why is this baptism necessary?
A2: To empower believers for witness, give boldness, grant victory over sin, release spiritual gifts, and deepen intimacy with God.

Q3: What is the evidence of Spirit baptism?
A3: In Acts, the initial sign was speaking in tongues, but the ongoing evidence is bold witness, holy living, and spiritual fruit (Acts 2:4; Galatians 5:22–23).

Q4: How can a believer receive the baptism?
A4: By thirsting for more of God, asking in faith, believing His promise, yielding fully, and receiving by the Spirit's power (Luke 11:13; Acts 2:4).

Q5: How should a Spirit-filled Christian live?
A5: By continually being filled, praying in the Spirit, walking in holiness, exercising spiritual gifts, and bearing bold witness to Christ.

Reflection Points

- Have I received the baptism of the Spirit since believing?
- Am I living in power or in weakness?
- Do I see evidence of the Spirit in my prayer, witness, and daily life?
- Have I allowed misconceptions or fear to block me from receiving?
- Am I continually being filled, or am I running on yesterday's experience?

Closing Prayer

Father, thank You for the promise of the Holy Spirit. Baptize me afresh with Your Spirit and with fire. Let every fear, doubt, and hindrance be removed. Fill me until I overflow with boldness, gifts, and fruit. Help me to live daily in the Spirit's power, to walk in holiness, and to witness with courage. May my life be a testimony that JESUS is alive and working in me. In His mighty name, Amen.

Chapter 24

Easter – The Power of the Resurrection

(Luke 24:5–6)

> *"And as they were afraid, and bowed down their faces to the earth, they said unto them, Why seek ye the living among the dead? He is not here, but is risen: remember how he spake unto you when he was yet in Galilee." (Luke 24:5–6 KJV)*

Introduction

Easter is not just a holiday, tradition, or seasonal festival — it is the foundation of Christian faith. Without the resurrection of Jesus Christ, the cross would be incomplete, faith would be empty, and salvation would be impossible. The resurrection is proof that Jesus is the Son of God, the Savior of the world, and the conqueror of death and the grave.

Paul declares: "If Christ be not raised, your faith is vain; ye are yet in your sins" (1 Corinthians 15:17). Easter is therefore not about eggs, rabbits, or cultural festivities, but about the risen Christ and the eternal victory He secured for us. It is the greatest event in history, transforming despair into hope, defeat into victory, and death into life.

The Prophetic Foundations of Easter

The resurrection was not an accident — it was foretold throughout Scripture:
- The Passover lamb in Exodus pointed to Christ, the Lamb of God who takes away the sins of the world (Exodus 12; John 1:29).
- David foresaw the resurrection: "For thou wilt not leave my soul in hell; neither wilt thou suffer thine Holy One to see corruption" (Psalm 16:10).
- Jesus Himself predicted His resurrection on the third day (Matthew 16:21; John 2:19).

Easter proves that God always keeps His promises.

The Meaning of Easter

- Easter celebrates the resurrection of Jesus Christ on the third day after His crucifixion (Matthew 28:1–6).
- It confirms God's power to bring life from death and hope from despair.
- It marks the turning point of history: sin defeated, Satan conquered, and eternal life secured.

Easter reminds us that the darkest Friday is always followed by the brightest Sunday.

The Power of the Resurrection

1. Victory Over Sin – Through His death and resurrection, Jesus broke sin's chains (Romans 6:6–10).
2. Victory Over Death – Death lost its sting and the grave lost its victory (1 Corinthians 15:55–57).
3. Assurance of Eternal Life – Because He lives, we shall live also (John 14:19).
4. Power for Daily Living – The same Spirit that raised Jesus empowers us to overcome weakness, fear, and temptation (Romans 8:11).
5. Boldness in Witness – The resurrection turned fearful disciples into fearless preachers (Acts 4:33).

The Empty Tomb – Evidence of Resurrection

The resurrection is not a myth but a historical event. God left witnesses:
- The women at the tomb (Matthew 28:1–10).
- The disciples who saw and touched Him (John 20:19–29).
- Over 500 witnesses at once (1 Corinthians 15:6).
- Transformed lives: fearful disciples became world changers, willing to die for what they saw.

The empty tomb is God's eternal testimony that death is defeated.

Living the Resurrection Life

Easter is not only about remembering what Christ did — it is about living in its reality:
- New Identity – We are risen with Christ (Colossians 3:1–3).
- New Purpose – We walk in newness of life (Romans 6:4).
- New Power – Resurrection power helps us overcome addiction, fear, and failure (Philippians 3:10).
- New Mission – We are called to proclaim the risen Christ to all nations (Matthew 28:18–20).

Living the resurrection life means refusing to live in defeat when Christ has secured our victory.

Easter and Our Hope

Easter anchors our hope in what is to come:
- Resurrection of the dead – The trumpet will sound, and the dead in Christ shall rise (1 Thessalonians 4:16).
- Immortality – Corruption shall put on incorruption (1 Corinthians 15:53).
- Eternal glory – We shall see Christ and be like Him (1 John 3:2).

Easter reminds us that our future is not a grave, but glory.

Interactive Q&A

Q1: What is the true meaning of Easter?
A1: It is the celebration of Christ's resurrection, proving His victory over sin, death, and the grave, and giving believers hope of eternal life.

Q2: Why is the resurrection central to Christianity?
A2: Without it, faith would be meaningless, forgiveness incomplete, and salvation impossible (1 Corinthians 15:17).

Q3: What evidence supports the resurrection?
A3: The empty tomb, eyewitnesses including the disciples and over 500 brethren, and transformed lives that prove the reality of the risen Christ.

Q4: How does the resurrection impact believers today?
A4: It gives us power to overcome sin, hope in trials, assurance of eternal life, and boldness to proclaim the gospel.

Q5: What future hope does Easter guarantee?
A5: The resurrection of all believers, eternal life with Christ, and ultimate victory over death forever.

Reflection Points

- Am I living in the victory of Easter, or still bound by sin and fear?
- Do I believe in the power of the resurrection for my daily struggles?
- How does Easter shape my response to suffering and trials?
- In what ways am I sharing the reality of the risen Christ with others?
- Does the hope of resurrection influence how I live today?

Closing Prayer

Lord Jesus, thank You for dying on the cross and rising again in victory. Thank You that the tomb is empty, and that death has been defeated. Help me to live daily in the reality of Your resurrection. Empower me by the Holy Spirit to overcome sin, fear, and despair. Let the hope of Easter guide my words, my actions, and my mission, until I see You face to face. In Your name, Amen.

Chapter 25

Training Up a Child in the Way of the Lord
(Proverbs 22:6)

"Train up a child in the way he should go: and when he is old, he will not depart from it." (Proverbs 22:6 KJV)

Introduction

Children are one of God's greatest gifts and greatest responsibilities. Proverbs 22:6 makes it clear that how we train our children determines the direction of their lives. Children are like soft clay — easy to shape in their early years, but hard to reshape when they become older. Whatever we plant in them early will grow with them and often stay with them for life.

This is why Christian parents must be intentional, consistent, and prayerful in raising their children in the way of the Lord. The devil desires to capture children early (Exodus 10:9–11), but God calls us to raise them as His disciples, not leaving even one behind.

The Power of Example

Training children goes beyond words. It is more about what we do than what we say. James reminds us: "Faith without works is dead" (James 2:26).

- Actions outweigh words – A child learns 80% from observation and 20% from instruction.
- Hypocrisy destroys training – Saying "don't lie" but lying in front of the child teaches lying.
- Parental conflicts leave scars – A father who shouts at or beats his wife teaches his son to abuse women and his daughter to distrust men. A mother who disrespects her husband teaches her children the same.
- Church and God's servants – Parents who constantly criticize the church and pastors in front of their children raise children who hate God's house.

Paul said, "Be ye followers of me, even as I also am of Christ" (1 Corinthians 11:1). The best training is a life of integrity, free of hypocrisy.

Discipline and Correction

Scripture is clear that correction is part of love:

- "He that spareth his rod hateth his son: but he that loveth him chasteneth him betimes" (Proverbs 13:24).
- "The rod and reproof give wisdom: but a child left to himself bringeth his mother to shame" (Proverbs 29:15).

But the rod does not mean harsh physical beating. Beating a child with sticks or objects is abusive and un-Christlike. The rod represents loving discipline — correction done firmly, but with care.

- Discipline must never be in anger – Correction done in hatred destroys, but correction in love builds.
- Discipline should fit the child – What works for one child may not work for another.
- Avoid emotional punishment – Refusing to speak to your child breeds bitterness, not wisdom.
- Correct and move on – Discipline should always end with reassurance of love.

Ephesians 6:4 warns fathers not to provoke their children to wrath but to bring them up in the nurture and admonition of the Lord.

Raising Children in the Way of the Lord

The only sure way to train children is in God's way:

- Teach them God's Word – Read Scripture together (Deuteronomy 6:6–7).
- Pray with and for them – Cover their hearts and future in prayer.
- Model a godly life – Let them see consistency in your worship, honesty, and faith.
- Commit them to God – Remember Hannah who dedicated Samuel to the Lord (1 Samuel 1:27–28).

The goal is not just well-behaved children, but disciples of Christ who will carry the faith into future generations.

Interactive Q&A

Q1: What does it mean to train up a child?
A1: It means to intentionally shape a child's character, habits, and faith through consistent teaching, discipline, and example (Proverbs 22:6).

Q2: Why is parental example so important in training?
A2: Because children learn more by watching than by hearing. Hypocrisy cancels words, but integrity reinforces them (James 2:26).

Q3: What is the biblical meaning of "the rod" in discipline?
A3: It symbolizes loving correction, not abusive beating. Discipline must be firm but always done in love, aiming to guide, not to harm (Proverbs 13:24; Ephesians 6:4).

Q4: What dangers arise when children are left undisciplined?
A4: They may grow up stubborn, selfish, and rebellious, bringing shame to their parents and dishonor to God (Proverbs 29:15).

Q5: How can Christian parents ensure their children grow in the Lord's way?
A5: By teaching Scripture, living out godly examples, praying with and for them, disciplining with love, and dedicating them to God's service.

Reflection Points

- Am I modeling godly behavior for my children, or do my actions contradict my words?
- Do I discipline my children with love or with anger?
- Am I consistently praying for my children and guiding them in God's Word?
- How can I better dedicate my home to raising children in the

Lord's way?
- What legacy of faith am I building for the next generation?

Closing Prayer

Heavenly Father, thank You for the gift of children. Help me to raise them in Your way, with love, integrity, and godly discipline. Forgive me where I have failed in example or correction. Fill me with wisdom, patience, and grace to train them faithfully. Let none of my children be lost to the world or to the devil. May they grow to know You, love You, and serve You all their days. In Jesus' mighty name, Amen.

Chapter 26

Grace, Not Competition
(Matthew 20:1–16)

"So the last shall be first, and the first last: for many be called, but few chosen."
(Matthew 20:16 KJV)

Introduction

The world is built on competition — businesses compete for customers, schools compete for ranking, athletes compete for medals, even families sometimes compete with one another. But in the kingdom of God, the principle is very different: we are not in competition.

In the parable of the labourers (Matthew 20:1–16), Jesus reveals the heart of God toward His people. He shows us that His blessings are not earned through human merit or comparison, but given out of His mercy and grace.

The Parable of the Labourers

- The householder represents God.
- The vineyard represents the kingdom.
- The workers represent us, the believers.
- The wage (a penny) represents God's promised reward of salvation and eternal life.

Five groups of workers were hired at different hours of the day, yet all received the same wage. Naturally, the first group felt cheated, but the master reminded them: "Didst not thou agree with me for a penny? ... Is thine eye evil, because I am good?" (vv. 13–15).

This parable reminds us that:
- God blesses people according to His sovereignty.
- His mercy covers lost years (Joel 2:25–27).
- Grace, not competition, defines the kingdom of God.

The Danger of Competition in the Church

Competition among believers is a sign of immaturity. Paul warns: "For ye are yet carnal: for whereas there is among you envying, and strife, and divisions, are ye not carnal, and walk as men?" (1 Corinthians 3:3).

Competition leads to:
- Jealousy – comparing gifts or success.
- Strife and quarrelling – fighting for recognition.
- Bitterness and malice – harbouring hatred.
- Backbiting and gossip – destroying one another secretly.
- Pride – seeking to outshine instead of to serve.

Galatians 5:19–21 warns that those who live in such things will not inherit the kingdom of God.

Diversity of Callings and Gifts

God has not called all of us to do the same thing in the same way:
- "To one he gave five talents, to another two, and to another one; to every man according to his several ability" (Matthew 25:15).
- "If any man minister, let him do it as of the ability which God giveth" (1 Peter 4:11).
- "Now ye are the body of Christ, and members in particular" (1 Corinthians 12:27).

Paul planted, Apollos watered, but it was God who gave the increase (1 Corinthians 3:6–7). In the body of Christ, no gift is superior, no role is insignificant, and no believer should despise another.

Grace for the Eleventh Hour

The last group of workers received the same reward as the first. Why? Because the master is merciful. This teaches us:
- It is never too late – God restores wasted years.
- Our reward is based on grace, not comparison – God sees our faithfulness, not our start time.
- Motives matter more than appearance – The woman cleaning toilets in humility may be greater in God's sight than the preacher seeking fame.

Chosen, Not Just Called

Jesus concludes: "For many be called, but few chosen" (Matthew 20:16).
- Called: everyone invited to serve in the vineyard.
- Chosen: those who remain faithful, humble, and obedient to the end.

Let us strive to be among the chosen few by serving with sincerity, avoiding jealousy, and walking in love.

Interactive Q&A

Q1: What do you learn from this parable of the labourers?
A1: That God rewards according to His grace, not human

comparison. His mercy reaches even those who come late, and no one has the right to envy another's blessing.

Q2: Was the householder right to pay all equally? Why?
A2: Yes. He kept His agreement with the first group and chose to be generous to the others. God's generosity cannot be limited by human fairness.

Q3: Are Christians in competition with each other?
A3: No. We are one body with different gifts. Competition leads to jealousy and division, but God calls us to unity and love (1 Corinthians 12:27–31).

Q4: What does "Many are called, but few chosen" mean?
A4: Many are invited to serve in God's kingdom, but only those who remain faithful, humble, and obedient are chosen to share in the eternal reward.

Q5: How can we avoid the spirit of competition?
A5: By focusing on our calling, celebrating others' success, living in humility, and remembering that God is the One who gives increase (1 Corinthians 3:7).

Reflection Points

- Do I secretly compete with others in ministry or life?
- Am I jealous when others are praised, promoted, or blessed?
- Do I celebrate the grace of God in others, or do I compare myself to them?
- Am I serving God for recognition, or for His glory?

- How can I grow into one of the "chosen few" who remain faithful to the end?

Closing Prayer

Father, thank You for Your mercy and grace. Forgive me for times I have compared myself to others or allowed jealousy to grow in my heart. Teach me to rejoice in Your blessings upon others and to serve You faithfully in my own calling. Keep me from the spirit of competition, and help me to walk in humility, love, and unity. Let me be among the chosen few who remain faithful until the end. In Jesus' name, Amen.

Chapter 27

Christ's Second Coming – The Last Prophecy

(1 Thessalonians 4:16–18)

> *"For the Lord himself shall descend from heaven with a shout, with the voice of the archangel, and with the trump of God: and the dead in Christ shall rise first: Then we which are alive and remain shall be caught up together with them in the clouds, to meet the Lord in the air: and so shall we ever be with the Lord. Wherefore comfort one another with these words." (1 Thessalonians 4:16–18 KJV)*

Introduction

The Bible is filled with prophecy. Many have already been fulfilled — the birth of Christ, His death and resurrection, the outpouring of the Spirit at Pentecost, the regathering of Israel — but one prophecy remains at the center of history's final chapter: the second coming of Jesus Christ.

This is the last prophecy. Every other end-time event — judgment day, Armageddon, the rapture, the resurrection, the destruction of the present earth, and the creation of a new heaven and new earth — flows out of this one reality: Christ is coming again.

Yet, despite its importance, this is one of the most ignored truths in our generation. Modern preaching often emphasizes personal success — steps to prosperity, marriage, or career — while neglecting the blessed hope of the believer. But without the second coming of Christ, Christianity is reduced to empty religion. Our true hope is not in riches, but in His return (Titus 2:13).

The Certainty of His Return

The promise of Christ's second coming is repeated throughout Scripture. It is not a hidden doctrine but a central truth.

- Acts 1:11 – The angels declared: "This same Jesus… shall

so come in like manner as ye have seen him go into heaven."
- Matthew 24:27 – Jesus warned that His return will be as visible as lightning across the sky.
- Revelation 1:7 – "Every eye shall see Him."
- Hebrews 9:28 – To those who wait for Him, He will appear the second time, bringing salvation.

Christ's return will not be symbolic, secret, or limited. It will be global, visible, and undeniable.

Misinterpretations and Deceptions

Over the centuries, false teachings have clouded this truth:
- Some claim He returned spiritually at Pentecost.
- Some claim He has appeared secretly in unknown places.
- Others dismiss His coming as allegory or myth.

But Jesus warned in Matthew 24:26: "If they shall say unto you, Behold, he is in the desert; go not forth: behold, he is in the secret chambers; believe it not."

When Christ comes again, the entire world will know. No one will need to announce it — His glory will fill the heavens.

Why the Delay?

Nearly 2,000 years have passed since the ascension. Some scoff and say, "Where is the promise of His coming?" (2 Peter 3:4).

Peter reminds us:
- With the Lord, one day is as a thousand years, and a thousand years as one day (2 Peter 3:8).
- God is not slow, but patient — not willing that any should perish (2 Peter 3:9).
- The delay is mercy, giving time for repentance before judgment.
- But the day will come suddenly, like a thief in the night (2 Peter 3:10).

God's seeming delay is not forgetfulness but grace.

What Will Happen When He Comes?

1. The Rapture of the Saints – The dead in Christ will rise, and living believers will be caught up to meet Him in the air (1 Thessalonians 4:16–17).
2. The Judgment of All Men – Christ will reward each according to his works (Matthew 16:27; Revelation 20:12).
3. The New Creation – The heavens and earth will be dissolved, and God will create a new heaven and earth where righteousness dwells (2 Peter 3:13; Revelation 21:1).

This is not myth or metaphor — it is the climax of God's plan.

The Comfort of His Coming

The second coming is not meant to terrify believers but to comfort and encourage us. Paul writes: "Wherefore comfort one another with these words" (1 Thessalonians 4:18).

- To the persecuted, His coming means justice.
- To the suffering, His coming means relief.
- To the faithful, His coming means reward.
- To all who believe, His coming means eternal fellowship with the Lord.

The cry of the early church must be ours: "Even so, come, Lord Jesus" (Revelation 22:20).

How Should We Live Until He Comes?

- Live in Holiness – Be spotless and blameless (2 Peter 3:14).
- Stay Watchful – Be ready, for the Son of Man comes at an hour you do not expect (Matthew 24:44).
- Encourage Others – Comfort one another with this hope (1 Thessalonians 4:18).
- Endure to the End – Only those who remain steadfast will be saved (Matthew 24:13).

- Focus on Eternity – Do not exchange your soul for temporary gain (Matthew 16:26).

The second coming is not just a doctrine to believe — it is a lifestyle to live.

Interactive Q&A

Q1: Why is Christ's second coming called the last prophecy?
A1: Because it is the final event that fulfills and concludes all other prophecies — judgment, resurrection, and the new creation.

Q2: Will His coming be secret or visible?
A2: Visible to all. Scripture says every eye shall see Him (Revelation 1:7).

Q3: Why does it seem delayed?
A3: God is patient, giving time for repentance. His delay is mercy, not forgetfulness (2 Peter 3:9).

Q4: What will happen when Christ returns?
A4: The rapture of the saints, the judgment of all men, and the creation of a new heaven and new earth.

Q5: How should believers prepare for His return?
A5: By living holy lives, staying watchful, encouraging one another, and enduring faithfully until the end.

Reflection Points

- Am I truly ready for Christ's return?
- Do I live with eternity in view, or am I distracted by the temporary?
- Am I warning others about the coming judgment?
- Do I comfort fellow believers with this blessed hope?
- If Christ came today, would He find me faithful?

Closing Prayer

Lord Jesus, thank You for the promise of Your return. Forgive me for the times I have lived carelessly as though this world were my home. Help me to live in holiness, steadfastness, and hope, always ready to meet You. Give me grace to endure to the end, courage to proclaim this truth, and a heart that cries daily, "Even so, come, Lord Jesus." Amen.

Chapter 28

End Time Signs and Precautions
(Matthew 24)

"And as he sat upon the mount of Olives, the disciples came unto him privately, saying, Tell us, when shall these things be? and what shall be the sign of thy coming, and of the end of the world?" (Matthew 24:3)

Introduction

Only those blinded by the love of this world would claim that it will never end. The reality of "the end" is undeniable — even human history, with its wars, disasters, and destructive weapons, points toward a climax. Today, mankind has created weapons capable of wiping out the earth many times over. This alone makes it reasonable to believe what Scripture has long declared: the end of this world is not a matter of "if" but "when."

The Bible does not leave us ignorant. It does not reveal the exact date — for Jesus said, "But of that day and hour knoweth no man, no, not the angels of heaven, but my Father only" (Matthew 24:36). Instead, God has given us signs to watch for, so that His people would not be caught unaware.

The end of this world is not the end of existence, but the end of the devil, his followers, and his system (2 Corinthians 4:4). For the righteous, it is the beginning of eternal fellowship with God (John 3:16).

Signs of the End Time (Matthew 24)

Jesus gave clear signs of the last days:
1. False Christs — "Many shall come in my name, saying, I am Christ; and shall deceive many."
2. Wars and rumors of wars — conflicts and unrest globally.
3. Famines, pestilences, and earthquakes in diverse places.
4. Persecution and hatred of believers.
5. Betrayal and offenses — people turning against each other.
6. False prophets and deception.
7. Abounding iniquity causing love to grow cold.
8. The gospel preached in all the world before the end comes (Matthew 24:14).

Daniel also added two remarkable signs:
- Increased travel — "many shall run to and fro."
- Explosion of knowledge — "knowledge shall be increased" (Daniel 12:4).

We are living in the very days Daniel foresaw: rapid global travel and a flood of knowledge in science and technology.

2. The Call for Precautions

The signs are not given to frighten believers, but to prepare them. Just as Noah was warned to build an ark (Genesis 6–7), so also we are given precautions for our time.

- Christ is our Ark. Unlike Noah, we don't build an ark — we enter the one God has already prepared: Jesus Christ (John 3:16).
- Be sober and vigilant (1 Thessalonians 5:6–8; 1 Peter 5:8).
- Be watchful and prepared like the wise virgins who had extra oil (Matthew 25:1–13). The oil represents holiness, righteousness, and readiness.
- Remain faithful — the Lord must find us serving, not beating our fellow servants or indulging in sin (Luke 12:42–48).
- Endure to the end — "he that shall endure unto the end, the same shall be saved" (Matthew 24:13).

The Final Sign: The Gospel Preached to All Nations

The final and ultimate sign of the end is this: "And this gospel of the kingdom shall be preached in all the world for a witness unto all nations; and then shall the end come" (Matthew 24:14).

Until this prophecy is fulfilled, the end will not come. This is why evangelism is not optional — it is central to God's plan. Every Christian must take the Great Commission seriously (Mark 16:15).

The devil knows this, which is why he works hard to silence the church, distract believers, and impose restrictions in nations. But Christ's command still stands: "Go ye into all the world, and preach the gospel to every creature."

Interactive Q&A

Q1: What does "the end of the world" mean in biblical context?
A1: It means the close of the present age and the destruction of the devil's system, followed by judgment and the establishment of God's eternal kingdom (2 Peter 3:7–10).

Q2: What are some key signs of the end time?
A2: False Christs, wars, natural disasters, persecution, false prophets, abounding sin, love growing cold, global travel,

increase of knowledge, and the worldwide preaching of the gospel (Matthew 24; Daniel 12:4).

Q3: What is the final sign before the end comes?
A3: The preaching of the gospel of the kingdom in all the world as a witness to all nations (Matthew 24:14).

Q4: What precautions should Christians take?
A4: Enter into Christ (the true Ark), live holy and watchful, keep extra oil of righteousness, remain faithful, and endure to the end (Matthew 25:1–13; 1 Thessalonians 5:6–8).

Q5: Why is evangelism central to the end time?
A5: Because the end will not come until the gospel is preached to all nations. Every believer must engage in the Great Commission (Mark 16:15).

Reflection Points

- Do I recognize the signs of the times, or am I distracted by the world?
- Am I living watchfully, soberly, and faithfully?
- Do I treat the Great Commission as my personal responsibility?
- If Christ came today, would He find me ready and serving?

Closing Prayer

Lord, thank You for not leaving us in darkness about the times. Help me to watch, to pray, and to remain faithful. Remove distractions from my heart and give me the oil of holiness and endurance. Use me to proclaim the gospel so that others may be ready for Your return. In Jesus' name, Amen.

Chapter 29

The Joy of the Lord: Your Strength
(Nehemiah 8:10)

"...for the joy of the LORD is your strength." (Nehemiah 8:10b)

Introduction

Joy is something every human being longs for. Yet people often search for it in fleeting places — parties, relationships, wealth, achievements, food, sex, travels, or possessions. These may offer moments of happiness, but they quickly fade.

True joy cannot be found in what you own or achieve. It is found only in the Lord. The Bible says: "The joy of the LORD is your strength." This is not ordinary joy; it is divine, unshakable, and eternal. It is the kind of joy that keeps you standing when life tries to break you.

Joy: A Gift from God

Nehemiah 8:10 reveals important truths about joy:
1. Joy is real — it is more than a passing emotion; it is a spiritual reality.
2. Joy has many sources — but most are temporary.
3. There is a unique joy — the joy of the Lord, flowing from His presence.
4. This joy strengthens — it empowers believers to endure trials, remain faithful, and overcome weakness.

The joy of the Lord is not something you create; it is something God gives. It is part of His nature shared with His people.

Temporary Joy vs. Eternal Joy

The first part of Nehemiah 8:10 encouraged God's people to celebrate with food, drink, and generosity. These are good and valid sources of joy. Fellowship, giving, holy living, and small blessings of life can bring happiness.

But Scripture shows that joy is ultimately a choice. You can choose to focus on your troubles, or you can choose to rejoice in God's goodness.

The prophet Habakkuk said: "Although the fig tree shall not blossom, neither shall fruit be in the vines… Yet I will rejoice in the LORD, I will joy in the God of my salvation" (Habakkuk 3:17–18). Even when nothing went right, he chose joy. This is the power of the joy of the Lord.

Joy Is a Command

God doesn't merely suggest joy — He commands it:
- "Rejoice evermore" (1 Thessalonians 5:16).
- "Break forth into joy" (Isaiah 52:9).
- "Rejoice in the Lord alway: and again I say, Rejoice" (Philippians 4:4).

Why? Because joy is not just for happiness; it is essential for spiritual health. A sad Christian is a weak Christian, but a joyful Christian is a strong one.

Joy Brings Strength

Sorrow weakens, but joy strengthens:
- Spiritually — Joy keeps you encouraged in trials; sorrow leads to discouragement.
- Physically — "A merry heart doeth good like a medicine"

(Proverbs 17:22). Joy promotes health.
- Emotionally — Joy brings resilience, while sorrow weighs down the spirit.

David testified: "Blessed is the people that know the joyful sound" (Psalm 89:15). Paul, even facing suffering, declared that his goal was to "finish my course with joy" (Acts 20:24).

Joy and the Holy Spirit

The joy of the Lord is not natural but supernatural. It is the fruit of the Holy Spirit:

"But the fruit of the Spirit is love, joy, peace, longsuffering, gentleness, goodness, faith…" (Galatians 5:22–23).

A Spirit-filled Christian will always reflect joy, even in hardship. You cannot separate joy from the presence of God. If joy is missing, it often means the believer has lost focus on Christ.

Choosing Joy Daily

Like salvation, joy is a personal choice. You may not control life's circumstances, but you can control your response to them. Joy is not based on events, possessions, or people — it is rooted in God Himself.

When sadness tries to creep in, you can choose joy by:

- Recalling God's past faithfulness — remember how He has brought you through before.

- Trusting His promises for the future — believe His Word even when circumstances look uncertain.

- Focusing on His Word and presence — meditate on Scripture and rest in God's nearness.

- Praying, singing, and giving thanks until heaviness lifts and peace returns.

The Bible says, "Break forth into joy" (Isaiah 52:9). That means you don't wait passively — you act in faith to push away sorrow and embrace God's gladness.

Isaiah declared: "I will greatly rejoice in the LORD, my soul shall be joyful in my God; for he hath clothed me with the garments of salvation" (Isaiah 61:10). Notice the phrase "I will" — joy is an intentional decision.

Interactive Q&A

Q1: What are some common sources of joy?
A1: Things like parties, wealth, achievements, relationships, and entertainment — but all are temporary.

Q2: Which source of joy is permanent?
A2: Only the joy of the Lord, rooted in His presence and salvation (Nehemiah 8:10).

Q3: What does "the joy of the Lord" mean?
A3: It is the supernatural joy that flows from God's Spirit, giving believers strength to endure and remain faithful.

Q4: Why is joy important for Christians?
A4: Because joy strengthens spiritually, physically, and emotionally, while sorrow weakens and discourages.

Q5: How can believers remain joyful when sadness comes?
A5: By choosing joy, recalling God's faithfulness, trusting His promises, focusing on His Word, and yielding to the Holy Spirit.

Reflection Points

- Am I looking for joy in temporary things or in the Lord?
- Do I truly see joy as my strength?
- How do I respond when heaviness and sorrow try to overwhelm me?
- Is joy visible in my life as evidence of the Holy Spirit?

- What practical step can I take today to break forth into joy and encourage others to rejoice in the Lord?

Closing Prayer

Father, thank You for the gift of joy that no circumstance can take away. Teach me to rejoice in You always. When sorrow tries to overwhelm me, remind me of Your faithfulness. Fill me with the joy of the Holy Spirit so that I may stand strong, live faithfully, and reflect Your goodness to the world. In Jesus' name, Amen.

Chapter 30

Love – The Greatest Commandment
(1 Corinthians 13)

> *"Though I speak with the tongues of men and of angels, and have not charity, I am become as sounding brass, or a tinkling cymbal." (1 Corinthians 13:1)*

Introduction

Love is the heartbeat of Christianity. Without love, all other virtues, gifts, and sacrifices lose their meaning. Paul reminds us in 1 Corinthians 13 that even the most impressive spiritual gifts, acts of faith, or sacrifices are worthless if they are not rooted in love.

The Greek word agape (translated "charity" in the KJV) means divine, unconditional love — the very nature of God Himself. To be a Christian is to live in love, for "God is love" (1 John 4:8).

Christianity Without Love is Empty

Paul gives three striking examples:
- Spiritual gifts without love — eloquence, prophecy, or tongues are just noise (vv.1–2).
- Faith without love — even faith that moves mountains is empty without love.
- Sacrifice without love — giving to the poor or even dying as a martyr profits nothing if done without love.

Love is not optional. Without it, everything collapses.

The Command to Love

Scripture is clear:
- "Beloved, let us love one another: for love is of God" (1 John 4:7).
- "If a man say, I love God, and hateth his brother, he is a liar" (1 John 4:20).
- "Follow peace with all men, and holiness, without which no man shall see the Lord" (Hebrews 12:14).

Jesus declared love to be the ultimate commandment:
- Love God with all your heart.
- Love your neighbor as yourself (Matthew 22:36–40).

This is the very requirement for eternal life (Luke 10:25–28).

What Love Looks Like

1 Corinthians 13:4–8 gives a checklist for genuine love:
- Love is patient and kind.
- Love is not jealous or boastful.
- Love is not proud, rude, or selfish.
- Love is not easily provoked and does not keep records of wrongs.
- Love rejoices in truth, not in evil.
- Love bears, believes, hopes, and endures all things.
- Love never fails.

This is the test of Christian maturity. Anything less is childish (1 Corinthians 13:11).

Love as the Mark of True Discipleship

Jesus said:
- "By this shall all men know that ye are my disciples, if ye have love one to another" (John 13:35).

- "This is my commandment, That ye love one another, as I have loved you" (John 15:12).

It is not church attendance, miracles, or titles that mark discipleship — it is love. Love is the ultimate witness to the world and the seal of true Christianity.

The Greatest of All

Paul concludes: "And now abideth faith, hope, charity, these three; but the greatest of these is charity" (1 Corinthians 13:13).

- Faith connects us to God.
- Hope anchors us for the future.
- Love reflects the very nature of God, and it will endure forever.

Love is heaven's language. Without it, no one will see God.

Interactive Q&A

Q1: What is love, and why is it essential to Christians?
A1: Love is the divine nature of God (agape), and without it Christianity is empty. It is the foundation of all Christian living (1 John 4:7–8).

Q2: What are the key attributes of love?
A2: Patience, kindness, humility, forgiveness, truthfulness, endurance, and unselfishness (1 Corinthians 13:4–8).

Q3: Can someone love God while hating their neighbor?
A3: No. Scripture says anyone who claims to love God but hates their brother is a liar (1 John 4:20).

Q4: Who are we commanded to love?
A4: Everyone — God, neighbors, friends, strangers, even enemies. Love is without boundaries (Matthew 5:44; Hebrews 12:14).

Q5: Why is love greater than faith and hope?
A5: Because love is eternal. Faith and hope serve their purpose now, but love never ends — it is the essence of God Himself (1 Corinthians 13:13).

Reflection Points

- Is my Christianity marked more by gifts, knowledge, or works than by love?
- Do I show love even to those who wrong me?
- Am I patient, kind, and forgiving in daily life?
- Can others see Jesus through my love?
- Do I treat love as the greatest commandment, or as optional?

Closing Prayer

Lord, teach me to love as You love. Remove bitterness, envy, and pride from my heart. Let patience, kindness, and forgiveness flow through me. Help me to love You fully and to love others without condition, so that my life reflects Christ. Amen.

Chapter 31

Prayer – The Lifeline of the Christian
(1 Thessalonians 5:17)

"Pray without ceasing." (1 Thessalonians 5:17)

Introduction

Do you truly pray without ceasing? Or do you barely pray at all? Many Christians struggle with prayer not because of lack of time or energy — after all, we find time for work, social media, or conversations — but because we lack understanding of what prayer really is, why it matters, and how to engage in it effectively.

The Bible warns that "my people are destroyed for lack of knowledge" (Hosea 4:6). When prayer is misunderstood, it feels like a burden; when prayer is rightly understood, it becomes a joy and necessity.

Jesus Himself prayed with such intensity that His sweat became like drops of blood (Luke 22:44). And when He asked His disciples to watch and pray, He considered one hour a "small" thing (Matthew 26:40). If Jesus saw prayer as essential, how much more should we?

This chapter will help you discover:
1. What prayer is.
2. Why you must pray.
3. How to pray effectively.
4. Why some prayers remain unanswered.

What is Prayer?

Many define prayer as petition, supplication, or making requests known to God. While these are aspects of prayer, they do not capture its fullness. Prayer is far more than a list of requests.

The Bible itself uses a metaphor to explain prayer: communication. God said: "Call unto me, and I will answer thee" (Jeremiah 33:3). Prayer is the communication line between you and God.

- Faith is the network. Just as a phone needs a signal to connect, prayer requires faith to connect to heaven.
- Prayer is interaction with God. It is how we commune with the Spirit, not just when we have requests, but at all times.
- Prayer is relationship. A father is grieved when his children never speak to him. Likewise, God delights in our constant communication with Him.

Prayer is not just about asking — it is about staying connected.

Reasons for Prayer

Why should Christians pray without ceasing? Scripture gives many reasons:

1. Communication with God — strengthening fellowship with your Father.
2. Permission — inviting God to intervene in earthly affairs. This world is given to men, but through prayer we yield it back to Him.
3. Acknowledgment — recognizing God as our source of help and blessing.
4. Supplication — presenting our personal requests to God.
5. Intercession — standing in the gap for others.
6. Proof of Faith — showing that we believe in His power and

promises.
7. Submission — yielding our will to His will.
8. Exercising Authority — enforcing victory over the enemy in Jesus' name.
9. Worship — adoring and glorifying God.
10. Spiritual Warfare — pulling down strongholds (2 Corinthians 10:4).
11. Renewal of the Mind — aligning our thoughts to Christ (2 Corinthians 10:5).

The Call to Pray Without Ceasing

Paul's instruction is simple: "Pray without ceasing." This does not mean spending 24 hours on your knees, but maintaining a constant spirit of prayer. It means living in continual awareness of God's presence — speaking to Him throughout the day, in the quiet moments, in the workplace, in trials, and in thanksgiving.

Daniel maintained a consistent prayer life, praying three times each day (Daniel 6:10). David also expressed his devotion to prayer, declaring, "Evening, and morning, and at noon, will I pray, and cry aloud: and he shall hear my voice" (Psalm 55:17). Likewise, Jesus often withdrew to solitary places to pray (Mark 1:35). These examples remind us that true prayer is not occasional—it is continual. David further reflected, "My knees are weak through fasting; and my flesh faileth of fatness" (Psalm 109:24), showing the depth of his commitment and the physical cost of his spiritual discipline. Genuine prayer flows from a consistent, disciplined, and heartfelt relationship with God.

When Prayers Seem Unanswered

Sometimes it feels like heaven is silent. Why? The Bible shows some reasons:
- Unrepented sin can hinder prayer (Psalm 66:18).
- Wrong motives can block answers (James 4:3).
- Unforgiveness can close the line (Mark 11:25).
- God's timing — some answers are delayed for His purpose (Daniel 10:12–13).
- Greater glory — sometimes "No" or "Wait" is God's better answer (2 Corinthians 12:7–9).

When prayers seem unanswered, do not quit. Keep praying, trust His wisdom, and align your heart with His will.

Interactive Q&A

Q1: What is prayer in simple terms?
A1: Prayer is communication with God — the spiritual line of connection between heaven and earth.

Q2: Why should Christians pray?
A2: To communicate with God, invite His intervention, grow

in fellowship, intercede for others, worship Him, and wage spiritual warfare.

Q3: How often should Christians pray?
A3: Without ceasing — maintaining a daily, continual spirit of prayer (1 Thessalonians 5:17).

Q4: Why are some prayers not answered?
A4: Because of sin, wrong motives, unforgiveness, or God's timing. Yet unanswered does not mean ignored.

Q5: What should a Christian do when prayers seem unanswered?
A5: Continue praying, trust God's wisdom, examine your heart, and remain steadfast in faith.

Reflection Points

- Is my prayer life consistent or occasional?
- Do I treat prayer as a relationship, or just a request list?
- Am I giving God permission to move in my life through prayer?
- When my prayers feel unanswered, do I trust His timing?
- Do I live with a spirit of prayer throughout the day?

Closing Prayer

Lord, thank You for the gift of prayer. Teach me to pray without ceasing, to remain connected to You at all times. Forgive me for neglecting prayer or treating it as a burden. Fill me with the Spirit of prayer and supplication so that my life will always reflect faith, intimacy, and submission to You. In Jesus' name, Amen.

Chapter 32

Make Hay While the Sun Shines – Avoiding Delay and Procrastination

(Proverbs 10:5; Ecclesiastes 3:1; Romans 12:11)

"He that gathereth in summer is a wise son: but he that sleepeth in harvest is a son that causeth shame." (Proverbs 10:5)

Introduction

"Make hay while the sun shines" is an old English proverb, but its truth is deeply biblical. It speaks of urgency, opportunity, and wisdom in action. In medieval times, farmers depended on the dry summer months to cut and preserve hay for their livestock. If they delayed, rain could ruin the harvest, leaving them and their animals hungry.

In life, just as in farming, there are windows of opportunity that do not stay open forever. To miss them is to face regret. Scripture emphasizes the same principle: Ecclesiastes 3:1, Romans 12:11. The sun will not shine forever. Time is passing. Youth, strength, opportunities, and even life itself are not permanent. That is why we must act now.

Understanding the Call of Wisdom

The proverb (Proverbs 10:5) contrasts two people:
- The wise son: gathers in summer, uses the right time, and plans ahead.
- The foolish son: sleeps in harvest, wastes opportunity, and brings shame.

God's wisdom is practical. He calls us to use time wisely (Ephesians 5:15–16). Wisdom is not only about knowing what is right but about doing it at the right time.

The Tragedy of Procrastination

Procrastination means delaying what should be done now. It is not just laziness — it can be fear, doubt, or misplaced priorities. But procrastination is dangerous because:

- Opportunities expire.
- Energy fades.
- Life is uncertain (Hebrews 9:27).

Many dreams are buried in graveyards — not because they were impossible, but because people said, "Tomorrow."

Biblical Warnings Against Delay

The Bible repeatedly warns against postponing:
- Salvation (2 Corinthians 6:2).
- Obedience: Pharaoh delayed and faced destruction (Exodus 9–12).
- Service: The slothful servant buried his talent and was cast into outer darkness (Matthew 25:24–30).

Delay can turn into disobedience.

Common Reasons for Procrastination

1. Laziness (Proverbs 6:9–11).
2. Fear of failure or the unknown (Joshua 1:9).
3. Distractions (Luke 8:14).
4. False confidence in tomorrow (James 4:13–15).
5. Perfectionism (Ecclesiastes 11:4).

Breaking Free from Procrastination

How do we make hay while the sun shines?
- Start today (Ecclesiastes 11:4).
- Set priorities (Matthew 6:33).
- Act in faith (Hebrews 13:21).
- Discipline yourself (Proverbs 12:24).
- Pray and act (James 2:26).

Practical Life Applications

- Spiritual life: Don't postpone repentance, prayer, Bible study, or evangelism.
- Education: Don't wait until exam day — start studying today.
- Family and marriage: Invest time and love now.
- Career and finances: Plan, save, and invest early.
- Health: Care for your body today, not tomorrow.

Interactive Q&A

Q1: What does "make hay while the sun shines" mean in biblical terms?
A1: It means seizing God-given opportunities and acting at the right time (Proverbs 10:5).

Q2: Which scriptures encourage us to act promptly?
A2: Ecclesiastes 3:1, Romans 12:11, 2 Corinthians 6:2, James

4:13–15.

Q3: What is procrastination, and why is it dangerous?
A3: It is delaying what should be done now; it is dangerous because opportunities expire, strength fades, and life is uncertain.

Q4: What are common reasons people procrastinate?
A4: Laziness, fear, distractions, misplaced priorities, false confidence in tomorrow, perfectionism.

Q5: How can believers overcome procrastination?
A5: By starting today, setting godly priorities, acting in faith, developing discipline, and combining prayer with action.

Reflection Points

- Am I delaying something God has already asked me to do?
- What excuses have I been using to justify procrastination?
- If today were my last day, what unfinished business would I regret?
- Do I treat my time as a gift from God or as something endless?
- What one step of action can I take today toward my calling?

Closing Prayer

Lord, deliver me from procrastination and slothfulness. Teach me to number my days, that I may apply my heart unto wisdom. Help me to seize every opportunity You place before me and to act with diligence and faith. May I never bring shame through delay but glorify You by making hay while the sun shines. In Jesus' name, Amen.

Chapter 33

Taming the Tongue: A Test of True Faith

(James 3:5)

"Even so the tongue is a little member, and boasteth great things. Behold, how great a matter a little fire kindleth!" (James 3:5 KJV).

Introduction

The tongue is one of the smallest parts of the human body, yet it carries extraordinary power. With it, destinies are shaped, lives are blessed, homes are built, and peace is preserved. With the same tongue, however, lives are destroyed, marriages are torn apart, churches are divided, and wars are ignited. James compares the tongue to a little spark that can set a whole forest ablaze (James 3:6).

Words matter. Words are not light things — they are seeds that carry consequences. A careless word can wound deeply, but a timely word can heal, uplift, and restore. Proverbs 18:21 says, "Death and life are in the power of the tongue: and they that love it shall eat the fruit thereof."

The Tongue Directs Destiny

James also likens the tongue to the bit in a horse's mouth and the rudder of a ship (James 3:3–4). Just as those small tools control mighty forces, so does the tongue control the course of a person's life.

- A careless remark can end a friendship.
- A harsh word can destroy a marriage.
- A lie can ruin a reputation.
- But likewise, a word of encouragement can save a soul from despair.

Your tongue can turn you toward life or toward destruction.

The Source of Words

Jesus said, "Out of the abundance of the heart the mouth speaketh" (Matthew 12:34). The tongue does not act alone; it is the mouthpiece of the heart. That means controlling the tongue begins with transforming the heart.

If the heart is full of anger, bitterness, or lust, those things will spill out through words. But if the heart is filled with God's Word, faith, and love, then life-giving words will flow out.

The Danger of the Tongue

James warns us that with the tongue:
- We bless God and yet curse men made in His image (James 3:9–10).
- We speak words that may lead to destruction or hell fire (Matthew 5:22).
- We will give an account for every idle word in the day of judgment (Matthew 12:36–37).

Proverbs 6:16–19 lists seven things God hates, and three of them are related to the tongue: a lying tongue, a false witness, and one who sows discord among brethren. That alone tells us how seriously God takes our words.

Controlling the Tongue

The Bible does not pretend that controlling the tongue is easy. James even calls it "an unruly evil, full of deadly poison" (James 3:8). But with God's help, it is possible.

Steps to Control the Tongue:
1. Discipline & Self-Control – "Be swift to hear, slow to speak" (James 1:19).
2. Integrity – Let your words be truthful, seasoned with grace (Colossians 4:6).
3. Prayer – Ask God, like David, "Set a watch, O LORD, before my mouth; keep the door of my lips" (Psalm 141:3).
4. Holy Spirit's Power – Only a Spirit-filled life can tame the tongue and use it for blessing.
5. Renewing the Heart – Fill your mind with God's Word, because what is inside will eventually come out.

Words that Heal, Not Harm

Instead of using the tongue to destroy, Christians are called to use it to:
- Bless and not curse (Romans 12:14).
- Encourage and build up others (1 Thessalonians 5:11).
- Speak truth in love (Ephesians 4:15).
- Proclaim the Gospel (Romans 10:9–10).

Let your words be like medicine, bringing healing to others (Proverbs 12:18).

Interactive Q&A

Q1: What is the meaning of "tongue" in this text?
A1: It refers not just to the physical organ, but to the words we speak — the expressions of the heart (Matthew 12:34).

Q2: How should a Christian use his or her tongue?
A2: To bless, encourage, pray, proclaim truth, and glorify God — never to curse, slander, or destroy (Ephesians 4:29).

Q3: How can one control his or her tongue?
A3: Through self-discipline, prayer, integrity, and the power of the Holy Spirit (Psalm 141:3; James 1:19).

Q4: Are prayers and deliverance needed for controlling the tongue?
A4: Yes. Since the tongue is connected to the heart, prayer, repentance, and sometimes deliverance are essential for lasting transformation.

Q5: What is the danger of using the tongue wrongly?
A5: It can lead to destroyed relationships, loss of opportunities, shame, judgment before God, and even eternal consequences (Matthew 12:36).

Reflection Points

- Do my words build up or tear down?
- Do I think before I speak, or do I speak impulsively?
- Are there relationships damaged because of careless words?
- Do my words reflect the presence of Christ in my life?
- Am I using my tongue as an instrument of blessing or destruction?

Closing Prayer

Lord, I surrender my tongue to You. Forgive me for every careless word I have spoken. Fill my heart with Your Word so that my mouth may overflow with life, blessing, and encouragement. Set a watch over my lips and teach me to use my tongue only for Your glory. In Jesus' name, Amen.

Chapter 34

Knowledge and Wisdom
(James 1:5)

"If any of you lack wisdom, let him ask of God, that giveth to all men liberally, and upbraideth not; and it shall be given him."
(James 1:5 KJV)

Introduction

Knowledge and wisdom are often confused, yet they are not the same. They are like identical twins — close in appearance but different in essence. Many people use the words interchangeably, but Scripture shows us a clear distinction:

- Knowledge is information — knowing facts, truths, or principles.
- Wisdom is the correct application of that knowledge in real life.

Someone may know the dangers of smoking (knowledge) yet continue to smoke. That person is not wise. A Christian may know Scripture by memory (knowledge) but fail to live by it in daily life. That Christian lacks wisdom. The Bible calls us not only to gain knowledge but also to seek wisdom, for wisdom is the principal thing (Proverbs 4:7).

The Difference Between Knowledge and Wisdom

Knowledge can be learned through study, teaching, and observation. It fills the mind with facts.
Wisdom comes from God. It enables a person to apply knowledge rightly, in truth, love, and righteousness.

Noah's generation had knowledge of the ark, but only Noah's family had the wisdom to enter it (Genesis 7:1–7). Many know about Jesus, but only those who follow Him walk in wisdom.

The Tragedy of Knowledge Without Wisdom

It is possible to be:
- A smoking doctor who knows the health risks.
- A bankrupt accountant who understands finance.
- A sinful pastor who preaches holiness.

Knowledge without wisdom leads to hypocrisy, destruction, and shame. The Bible warns that knowledge alone "puffeth up" (1 Corinthians 8:1), but wisdom builds up.

Two Types of Wisdom

James distinguishes two kinds of wisdom (James 3:15–17):

1. Earthly Wisdom – "sensual, devilish," often used for selfish advantage, manipulation, or deceit. It is rooted in pride and dishonesty. Christians must reject it.
   - Example: a businessman who tricks his clients.
   - Example: a spouse who manipulates in marriage.

2. Godly Wisdom – "pure, peaceable, gentle, full of mercy, without hypocrisy." This is wisdom from above, rooted in the fear of the Lord (Proverbs 9:10). It brings peace, righteousness, and guidance in decisions.

Wisdom: A Gift from God

The Bible makes it clear: wisdom comes from God. We cannot manufacture it ourselves. That is why James encourages believers to ask God for wisdom, and He promises to give it generously (James 1:5).

Solomon understood this. When God offered him anything, Solomon asked for wisdom. As a result, God gave him wisdom, and along with it, riches and honor (1 Kings 3:9–13).

Jesus Himself "increased in wisdom and stature, and in favour with God and man" (Luke 2:52). If Christ prioritized wisdom, how much more should we?

The Balance of Knowledge and Wisdom

We must not despise knowledge, for "my people are destroyed for lack of knowledge" (Hosea 4:6). Knowledge and wisdom work together:
- Knowledge gives us light.
- Wisdom shows us how to walk in that light.

A believer who ignores knowledge will stumble in ignorance. A believer who ignores wisdom will stumble in foolishness. Both are necessary.

Practical steps:
- Acquire knowledge by studying Scripture, reading, learning,

and listening.
- Seek wisdom by praying, fearing God, and applying His Word daily.

Interactive Q&A

Q1: What is the difference between knowledge and wisdom?
A1: Knowledge is information and understanding, while wisdom is the correct application of that knowledge in life (Proverbs 4:7).

Q2: How many types of wisdom exist and what are the differences?
A2: Two. Earthly wisdom (selfish, manipulative, devilish – James 3:15) and godly wisdom (pure, peaceable, righteous – James 3:17).

Q3: What should a Christian do if he or she lacks wisdom?
A3: Ask God in prayer, for He gives wisdom generously without finding fault (James 1:5).

Q4: Should a Christian despise knowledge?
A4: No. Knowledge is essential. Without it, people perish (Hosea 4:6). But knowledge must be combined with wisdom to be fruitful.

Q5: How can someone acquire knowledge?
A5: By studying Scripture, learning from teachers, reading, meditating on God's Word, and being attentive to life lessons — then applying them with wisdom.

Reflection Points

- Do I merely know about God's Word, or do I live it out in wisdom?
- Have I been guilty of using earthly wisdom for selfish gain?
- Am I asking God daily for wisdom as James 1:5 instructs?
- Do I balance knowledge with wisdom, or do I lean to one side?
- How can I apply what I know today in a way that glorifies Christ?

Closing Prayer

Heavenly Father, thank You for the gift of knowledge and the greater gift of wisdom. Forgive me for times I have known the truth but failed to live it out. Fill me with wisdom from above that is pure and peaceable. Help me to apply what I know so that my life reflects Christ. May my decisions and actions bring glory to Your name. In Jesus' name, Amen.

Chapter 35

Knowledge, Understanding, and Wisdom

(Proverbs 2:6; James 1:5; Proverbs 4:7)

"For the LORD giveth wisdom: out of his mouth cometh knowledge and understanding." (Proverbs 2:6)

Introduction

Knowledge, understanding, and wisdom are three treasures that every believer must seek. They are often mentioned together in Scripture, but they are not the same. They are like three pillars supporting the house of a godly life.

Knowledge is the foundation, understanding is the structure, and wisdom is the roof that provides covering and direction. Without one, the building is incomplete.

Many people mistake knowledge for wisdom or confuse understanding with both. But the Bible makes it clear: it is not enough to know; one must understand, and not enough to understand; one must apply.

Knowledge — The Foundation of Truth

Knowledge is simply awareness of facts, truth, or principles. It comes by learning, reading, and listening. The Bible says: "My people are destroyed for lack of knowledge" (Hosea 4:6). Ignorance is deadly, both physically and spiritually.

Biblical Example: The Israelites had knowledge of God's law given through Moses. They knew His commandments, yet many perished in disobedience. Knowledge without obedience profits little.

Modern Example: A medical doctor knows smoking destroys the lungs. Yet, if he smokes, his knowledge does not save him.

Knowledge is good, but it must not stop at information. It must lead to understanding.

Understanding — The Insight of Meaning

Understanding is deeper than knowledge. It is discernment — the ability to grasp the meaning and purpose behind what is known. Proverbs 4:7 says, "Wisdom is the principal thing; therefore get wisdom: and with all thy getting get understanding."

Biblical Example: The men of Issachar were praised because they "had understanding of the times, to know what Israel ought to do" (1 Chronicles 12:32). Many in Israel had knowledge of the law, but only those with understanding could discern God's timing and direction.

Illustration: Many knew Noah was building an ark. They had knowledge of the project. But only Noah and his family understood why it mattered. Understanding led them inside the ark.

Understanding makes knowledge practical and prepares the way for wisdom.

Wisdom — The Application of Truth

Wisdom is the highest stage: the right application of knowledge and understanding. Wisdom is living by the truth you know and understand.

Biblical Example: Solomon, when given the chance to ask for anything, requested wisdom (1 Kings 3:9). Because he asked for wisdom, God gave him riches and honor as well.

Contrast Example: Judas Iscariot had knowledge of Jesus' teaching and even the privilege of being among the twelve. He saw miracles firsthand, yet lacked wisdom to follow truth. His end was destruction.

James 1:5 tells us to ask God for wisdom because it is not naturally produced. It is a gift from above.

Earthly vs. Godly Wisdom

The Bible distinguishes between two types of wisdom:

- Earthly Wisdom: manipulative, selfish, deceitful. James 3:15 calls it "earthly, sensual, devilish." This so-called wisdom tricks, flatters, or cheats for gain.
- Godly Wisdom: pure, peaceable, merciful, without hypocrisy (James 3:17). It builds rather than destroys, unites rather than divides.

Christians must avoid earthly wisdom and embrace the wisdom that comes from God alone.

How the Three Work Together

Think of these as steps:
1. Knowledge tells you what to do.
2. Understanding tells you why it matters.
3. Wisdom tells you how and when to do it.

Example:
- Knowledge: "Prayer is powerful."
- Understanding: "Prayer connects me with God and brings change."
- Wisdom: "Therefore, I will pray consistently, with faith, and in the Spirit."

Without knowledge, you perish. Without understanding, you misinterpret. Without wisdom, you misapply.

The Fear of the Lord — The True Beginning

"The fear of the LORD is the beginning of wisdom: and the knowledge of the holy is understanding" (Proverbs 9:10).

This means the starting point for all three is reverence for God. Without Him, knowledge puffs up, understanding is darkened, and wisdom turns corrupt.

Practical Keys to Grow in Knowledge, Understanding, and Wisdom

- Study the Word: Knowledge comes by learning (2 Timothy 2:15).
- Seek Insight: Meditate on Scripture and ask God for understanding (Psalm 119:34).
- Pray for Wisdom: James 1:5 assures us God will give it

liberally.
- Walk in Obedience: Application brings wisdom (Matthew 7:24).
- Learn from Others: Godly counsel sharpens wisdom (Proverbs 11:14).

Interactive Q&A

Q1: What is the difference between knowledge, understanding, and wisdom?
A1: Knowledge is knowing truth, understanding is grasping its meaning, and wisdom is applying it correctly.

Q2: How many kinds of wisdom exist?
A2: Two: earthly wisdom (selfish, devilish) and godly wisdom (pure, peaceable, from above).

Q3: What should a Christian do if he lacks wisdom?
A3: Ask God in prayer, who gives generously (James 1:5).

Q4: Should a Christian despise knowledge?
A4: No. Knowledge is essential, but it must lead to understanding and wisdom. Without knowledge, people perish (Hosea 4:6).

Q5: Why is the fear of the Lord the beginning of wisdom?
A5: Because it positions us in humility and dependence on God, the true source of all knowledge, understanding, and wisdom.

Reflection Points

- Do I only seek knowledge, or do I pursue understanding and wisdom as well?
- In what areas of my life am I failing to apply the wisdom I already know?
- Have I been relying on earthly wisdom instead of godly wisdom?
- Do my daily decisions reflect the fear of the Lord?
- How can I grow practically this week in knowledge, understanding, and wisdom?

Closing Prayer

Lord, grant me knowledge of Your truth, understanding of Your ways, and wisdom to apply them rightly. Deliver me from earthly wisdom, and fill me with the wisdom that comes from above. Let my life reflect You in thought, word, and action. In Jesus' name, Amen.

Chapter 36

Sowing and Reaping

(Galatians 6:7)

"Be not deceived; God is not mocked: for whatsoever a man soweth, that shall he also reap." (Galatians 6:7 KJV)

Introduction

Life operates under divine laws that cannot be altered. One of the greatest and most universal of these is the law of sowing and reaping. It is both spiritual and natural, applying to every area of life. You cannot escape it, override it, or bend it in your favor. It is God's way of ensuring justice and accountability in creation.

Whatever you sow is what you will reap. This principle applies to seeds in the ground, words from your mouth, attitudes in your relationships, and spiritual investments you make in the kingdom of God. Your present harvest is a reflection of yesterday's seeds, and your future harvest will reflect the seeds you plant today.

The Universality of the Law

This law transcends time, race, culture, and religion. Farmers know it: plant corn and reap corn; plant mango and reap mango. Spiritually, morally, and socially, it is the same. Sow kindness, and you reap kindness. Sow hatred, and you reap hatred.

Genesis 8:22 confirms it: 'While the earth remaineth, seedtime and harvest, and cold and heat, and summer and winter, and day and night shall not cease.' God established this principle at creation, and it has never failed.

The Type, Quality, and Quantity of Seeds Matter

- Type: You cannot sow evil and expect to reap good (Proverbs 22:8).
- Quality: Rotten seeds produce a rotten harvest; pure seeds produce good fruit (Matthew 7:17–18).

- Quantity: 'He which soweth sparingly shall reap also sparingly; and he which soweth bountifully shall reap also bountifully' (2 Corinthians 9:6).

Seeds Beyond the Soil

Sowing and reaping goes far beyond agriculture. Our entire lives are gardens, and we sow daily through:
- Our Words: 'Death and life are in the power of the tongue' (Proverbs 18:21).
- Our Actions: Acts of kindness, love, and generosity return multiplied (Luke 6:38).
- Our Choices: Laziness reaps poverty; diligence reaps abundance (Proverbs 10:4–5).
- Our Spiritual Walk: Sow to the Spirit, reap life; sow to the flesh, reap corruption (Galatians 6:8).

Taking Responsibility

This law emphasizes personal responsibility. Many blame others — parents, government, environment, or even the devil — but the truth is that much of life's harvest is a direct result of our own sowing.

- In Marriage: Sow love, forgiveness, and respect, and you reap peace and harmony. Sow bitterness, criticism, and neglect, and you reap strife.

- In Career or Business: Sow diligence, discipline, and excellence, and you reap success. Sow laziness, shortcuts, and dishonesty, and you reap failure.
- In Spiritual Life: Sow prayer, fasting, holiness, and the Word, and you reap strength and victory. Sow negligence, worldliness, and compromise, and you reap weakness and defeat.

Though life has unpredictable storms (the 20% beyond our control), the majority of outcomes (the 80%) are determined by our seeds.

Sowing and Reaping in Scripture

- Job: 'They that plow iniquity, and sow wickedness, reap the same' (Job 4:8).
- Hosea: 'They have sown the wind, and they shall reap the whirlwind' (Hosea 8:7).
- Paul: 'For the wages of sin is death; but the gift of God is eternal life through Jesus Christ our Lord' (Romans 6:23).
- Jesus: 'For with the same measure that ye mete withal it shall be measured to you again' (Luke 6:38).

Eternal Implications

The law of sowing and reaping extends beyond this world. Every action has eternal weight. Paul warns:

'For he that soweth to his flesh shall of the flesh reap corruption; but he that soweth to the Spirit shall of the Spirit reap life everlasting.' (Galatians 6:8)

This makes sowing and reaping not just a life principle but a salvation principle. What we sow spiritually determines where we will spend eternity.

Interactive Q&A

Q1: What do you understand by the law of sowing and reaping?
A1: It is the principle that whatever you sow, in word, deed, or spirit, you will reap in due time (Galatians 6:7).

Q2: Do you believe this law is universal? Why?
A2: Yes. It applies in agriculture, relationships, finances, health, and spirituality. It is a natural and spiritual law established by God (Genesis 8:22).

Q3: What lessons can we learn from this law?
A3: That we are largely responsible for our results in life, and that our future depends on the quality, type, and quantity of seeds we plant today.

Q4: What kinds of seeds should Christians sow?
A4: Seeds of love, holiness, generosity, truth, kindness, faith, and obedience to God's Word (James 3:18; Galatians 6:9–10).

Q5: What are the harvests of good and evil seeds?
A5: Good seeds produce blessings, peace, prosperity, and eternal life, while evil seeds produce sorrow, regret, destruction, and eternal separation from God (Romans 6:23).

Reflection Points

- What seeds am I sowing daily with my words, actions, and attitudes?
- Am I sowing into the Spirit or into the flesh?
- Do I take responsibility for my current harvest, or do I blame others?
- Am I sowing good seeds into my family, work, and spiritual life?
- What eternal harvest am I preparing for myself?

Closing Prayer

Heavenly Father, thank You for teaching me the principle of sowing and reaping. Forgive me for every wrong seed I have planted. Help me to sow righteousness, kindness, and faith, so that I may reap a harvest of peace and eternal life. Keep me mindful of my choices each day, and give me the grace to always sow to the Spirit. In Jesus' name, Amen.

Chapter 37

Unforgiveness – The Enemy of Progress
(Matthew 6:12)

"And forgive us our debts, as we forgive our debtors." (Matthew 6:12 KJV)

Introduction

Unforgiveness is one of the most dangerous enemies of progress in the Christian life. It destroys peace, blocks prayers, weakens faith, and even hinders salvation. Jesus considered forgiveness so vital that He included it in the model prayer He gave to His disciples. Immediately after teaching the Lord's Prayer, He emphasized that our forgiveness from God is directly connected to our willingness to forgive others (Matthew 6:14–15). To hold onto grudges is to chain ourselves to the past while trying to move into the future. Unforgiveness is not simply a bad habit — it is sin. It grieves the Holy Spirit, poisons relationships, and leaves the heart vulnerable to bitterness and Satan's deception.

The Command to Forgive

Forgiveness is not optional for Christians — it is a command. Jesus said:

"For if ye forgive men their trespasses, your heavenly Father will also forgive you: But if ye forgive not men their trespasses, neither will your Father forgive your trespasses." (Matthew 6:14–15).

If we refuse to forgive, we are refusing God's own mercy. Without forgiveness, there is no fellowship with Him, no answered prayers, and no hope of heaven.

Forgiveness Without Limits

When Peter asked if forgiving seven times was enough, Jesus replied, "Until seventy times seven" (Matthew

18:22). The number 490 is not literal — it means forgiveness should be without limits.

Jesus then illustrated with the parable of the unforgiving servant (Matthew 18:23–35). A servant forgiven a massive debt refused to forgive a small debt from a fellow servant. His master became angry and punished him. Jesus ended with a warning: "So likewise shall my heavenly Father do also unto you, if ye from your hearts forgive not every one his brother their trespasses."

Forgiveness must come from the heart, not just the lips.

The Bondage of Unforgiveness

Unforgiveness is like drinking poison and expecting the other person to die. It keeps you in pain while the offender may have forgotten and moved on.

Unforgiveness leads to:
- Bitterness that consumes the heart.
- Emotional pain that steals joy and peace.
- Physical sickness such as stress and high blood pressure.
- Spiritual weakness, unanswered prayers, and separation from God.

Some cannot even forgive themselves for past mistakes. But if God has forgiven you through Christ, you must also forgive yourself.

The Blessing of Forgiveness

Forgiveness does not excuse sin, but it frees you from bondage. It restores your fellowship with God, heals relationships, and opens the door for peace, joy, and answered prayer.

Ephesians 4:30–32 commands us to let go of all bitterness, wrath, and anger, and to forgive one another "even as God for Christ's sake hath forgiven you." Forgiveness brings progress, while unforgiveness keeps you stagnant and bitter.

Interactive Q&A

Q1: What is forgiveness, and what is unforgiveness?
A1: Forgiveness is releasing others from debt and letting go of resentment. Unforgiveness is holding onto grudges, anger, and bitterness.

Q2: What should be a Christian's attitude toward forgiveness?
A2: Forgiveness must be quick, complete, and from the heart. A Christian cannot afford to delay or place conditions on forgiveness (Ephesians 4:32).

Q3: How many times should we forgive?
A3: Always. Jesus said forgiveness has no limit — "seventy times seven" (Matthew 18:22).

Q4: What are the dangers of unforgiveness?
A4: It brings bitterness, emotional pain, sickness, broken fellowship with God, unanswered prayers, and eternal loss.

Q5: Can a Christian with an unforgiving heart make heaven?
A5: No. Jesus clearly taught that God will not forgive us if we refuse to forgive others (Matthew 6:14–15). Forgiveness is a command of Christ and a mark of true discipleship.

Reflection Points

- Am I carrying grudges against anyone from my past or present?
- Do I understand that my forgiveness from God depends on my willingness to forgive others?
- Have I truly forgiven from the heart, or just with my lips?
- Do I keep remembering wrongs instead of letting go?
- How can I practice forgiveness daily in my family, church, and relationships?

Closing Prayer

Lord, I thank You for forgiving me through Christ. Search my heart and remove every root of bitterness or unforgiveness. Help me to forgive others from the heart, just as You forgave me. Teach me to walk in love and mercy daily, so I may live in freedom and reflect Your character. In Jesus' name, Amen.

Chapter 38

The Rebellious Child and the Compassionate Father: Sin, Repentance, and Restoration

(Luke 15:11–32)

> *"And he said, A certain man had two sons: And the younger of them said to his father, Father, give me the portion of goods that falleth to me. And he divided unto them his living." (Luke 15:11–12 KJV)*

Introduction

This parable, commonly known as the prodigal son, is one of the most powerful illustrations of God's love in the entire Bible. However, calling it "the prodigal son" focuses attention only on reckless spending, as if the son would have been good had he wisely invested his inheritance. But the deeper truth is that he was a rebellious child regardless of how he spent the money, and his father was a compassionate father regardless of the rebellion.

This story is not primarily about money — it is about relationship, rebellion, repentance, and restoration. It is a mirror of our own lives when we rebel against God, and a portrait of the Father's unchanging compassion toward His children.

The Child's Rebellion

The younger son was impatient and self-centred. He could not wait for his father's natural timing, but demanded his share of the estate. This reveals a heart that wanted the father's blessings but not the father's presence — a picture of many today who want God's gifts but not His lordship.

He went into a far country, which symbolizes separation from God. There he wasted everything in reckless living. Soon, famine came, and the once-privileged son was reduced to feeding swine — a humiliating job for a Jew. He was so destitute that he desired the pigs' food.

Rebellion always leads to ruin. Sin may promise freedom, but it delivers slavery. Like Adam hiding from God after the fall, or Jonah swallowed by the fish, sin alienates us from the Father's presence.

Coming to Himself

Verse 17 says: "And when he came to himself..." This is the turning point. Every sinner must come to this moment of realization. The young man remembered that even his father's servants were better off than he was. He resolved to return home, confess his sin, and ask for mercy.

Repentance begins when we recognize our emptiness without God and make the choice to return to Him.

The Father's Compassion

While the son was still a long way off, the father saw him and ran to meet him. In Jewish culture, fathers did not run — but love made him run. He embraced his filthy son and restored him with robe, ring, shoes, and a feast.

This is God's heart toward us. He does not wait with folded arms; He runs toward us with mercy. Heaven rejoices when even one sinner repents (Luke 15:7).

Why We Must Avoid Sin and Rebellion

This parable also teaches us that even though God forgives, rebellion leaves scars. Seven reasons to avoid sinful living:

1. Scars remain — Sin may be forgiven, but its scars often linger (David's sin with Bathsheba, 2 Samuel 11).
2. Consequences follow — Forgiveness does not erase natural consequences (Galatians 6:7).
3. Frustration and shame — Sin brings confusion and disgrace, as seen in Adam, Eve, and this son (Proverbs 14:34).
4. Loss of God's presence — Rebellion separates us from the Father's covering.
5. Death — "The wages of sin is death" (Romans 6:23).
6. Exclusion from the Kingdom — Sin without repentance shuts people out of heaven (1 Corinthians 6:9–10).
7. God's displeasure — Sin provokes God's anger (Psalm 7:11).

Sin never leaves life better than it found it.

God, the Compassionate Father

Yet the story does not end with the son's rebellion but with the father's compassion. God is that compassionate Father. Our rebellion does not diminish Him — He remains holy, sovereign, and complete. But His love longs to restore us.

Like the father in the parable, God is ready to forgive, accept, and celebrate anyone who turns back to Him. He takes no pleasure in the death of a sinner but desires all to repent and live (Ezekiel 33:11; 2 Peter 3:9).

Interactive Q&A

Q1: What is the deeper meaning of this parable?
A1: It is about a rebellious child (humanity) and a compassionate Father (God) who restores the repentant.

Q2: What happens when someone lives in rebellion against God?
A2: They face shame, emptiness, separation from God, and ultimately death (Romans 6:23).

Q3: Why must we avoid sin even if God forgives?
A3: Because sin leaves scars, brings consequences, and robs us of peace, joy, and divine protection.

Q4: What does the father's response teach us about God?
A4: That He is merciful, compassionate, and quick to restore those who repent (Psalm 103:8–12).

Q5: What does God desire from sinners?
A5: Repentance and a return to Him, so they may experience forgiveness, restoration, and eternal life.

Reflection Points

- Do I ever desire God's blessings more than His presence?
- Have I "gone into a far country" in any area of my life?
- Do I believe God will truly accept me if I repent?
- Am I aware of the scars and consequences of rebellion?

- How can I show the Father's compassion to others who are struggling?

Closing Prayer

Father, thank You for being the compassionate One who runs to meet us when we turn back to You. Forgive us for our rebellion and help us never to stray from Your presence. Heal the scars of our past and give us the grace to walk in obedience. May our lives reflect Your mercy so others may also return home to You. In Jesus' name, Amen.

Chapter 39

Jesus: The Way, The Truth, and The Life
(John 14:6)

"Jesus saith unto him, I am the way, the truth, and the life: no man cometh unto the Father, but by me." (John 14:6)

Introduction

No statement in all of human history compares to the words Jesus spoke in John 14:6. When He declared, "I am the way, the truth, and the life," He uttered a statement so profound that no man born of a woman has ever dared to say anything like it. Kings, prophets, philosophers, and teachers have spoken wise words, but none have ever claimed to be the way, the truth, and the life.

Why? Because no one else has the authority to make such a claim. I don't have that authority, and no human being ever will. Only Jesus could speak these words with divine authority because He is not merely a man — He is the eternal Son of God. His words carry the weight of Heaven.

Throughout history, many religious leaders have pointed to paths, ideas, or philosophies they believed could lead to God. But Jesus does something different: He doesn't point to a way — He points to Himself. He says, "I am the way." That is what makes Christianity unique and what makes Jesus incomparable. Other religions may acknowledge Him as a prophet, a teacher, or a moral example, but Jesus declares that He alone is the exclusive path to the Father.

This one verse sums up the entire gospel message — Jesus is our way back to God, the absolute truth that sets us free, and the very source of eternal life.

Jesus Is the Way — The Only Path to God

In this world, many claim to know "a way" to God. Some believe good works will save them; others think that sincere devotion to religion is enough. But Jesus makes it clear — "No man cometh unto the Father, but by Me."

This is not arrogance; it is truth. It's not pride; it's divine revelation. Jesus is not one among many roads — He is the only road. He did not come to show us the way; He is the Way.

Humanity lost its way in Eden when sin separated man from God. Since then, people have tried in vain to find their way back through rituals, laws, and philosophies. But none of these could bridge the gap. Only Jesus could — and He did, through His death and resurrection.

When He stretched out His hands on the Cross, He bridged Heaven and earth. The cross became the doorway through which man could return to fellowship with God. That is why Hebrews 10:19–20 calls it "a new and living way" which He consecrated for us through His blood.

Every other way leads to confusion and destruction, but the way of Jesus leads to peace, purpose, and eternal destiny. To walk in His way is to walk in love, obedience, and holiness.

To truly say "Jesus is my way" means He guides your decisions, directs your path, and defines your purpose. You no longer wander in uncertainty — you walk in His light.

Jesus Is the Truth — The Final and Absolute Reality

In a world that questions everything and believes anything, Jesus stands as the unshakable Truth. He doesn't merely tell the truth — He embodies it. His nature, His words, and His works all reveal who God truly is.

Many have claimed to possess truth, but their teachings change with time. Jesus' truth never changes because it is eternal. He is the same yesterday, today, and forever (Hebrews 13:8). His truth exposes lies, corrects error, and reveals the reality of who we are and who God is.

When Pilate asked, "What is truth?" (John 18:38), the answer was standing right before him — Truth in the flesh.

Knowing Jesus means knowing truth that sets you free — free from sin, fear, deception, and confusion. Every lie of the enemy loses power when confronted by the light of Christ. That's why John 8:32 says, "Ye shall know the truth, and the truth shall make you free."

All human wisdom must bow before the truth of God's Word. The doctrines of men can be debated, but the truth of Christ cannot be shaken. When you build your life on the foundation of Jesus' truth, storms may come, but you will stand firm (Matthew 7:24–25).

Truth is not relative. Truth is not changing. Truth is a Person — and that Person is Jesus Christ.

Jesus Is the Life — The Source and Sustainer of All Things

Every living thing draws breath from the One who gave life. Jesus said, "I am come that they might have life, and that they might have it more abundantly." (John 10:10).

He is not speaking of mere existence. The life Jesus gives is Zoe — the divine life of God that fills the believer with spiritual vitality, peace, and strength.

Outside of Christ, humanity exists but does not truly live. Sin brings death, separation, and emptiness, but Jesus brings restoration, reconciliation, and eternal joy.

In John 11:25, Jesus said, "I am the resurrection and the life." Death itself must bow before Him. His life is not only eternal but also victorious. The same Spirit that raised Jesus from the dead dwells in us (Romans 8:11). That means the life of God now flows in every believer.

This life transforms us from within — changing our hearts, renewing our minds, and empowering us to walk in righteousness. It gives us the strength to overcome temptation, the courage to face trials, and the hope to endure every storm.

The life of Jesus is not temporary or fragile; it is eternal and unbreakable. It is the power of resurrection life at work in every believer.

The Unmatched Authority of Jesus' Words

When Jesus said, "I am the way, the truth, and the life," He spoke with authority that no human can imitate. No prophet, no priest, no philosopher, and no founder of any religion has ever claimed to be all three — the way, the truth, and the life — because no one else can.

Others may point to God; Jesus is God revealed in flesh. Others may speak about light; Jesus is the Light of the world. Others may promise life; Jesus gives life because He is life.

The boldness of His words reveals His divine identity. It takes God Himself to declare what only God can fulfill. He alone has the authority to forgive sins, to give eternal life, and to judge the world.

Even when many religions try to explain spiritual truth, they all, in some way, point back to Jesus — as a teacher, prophet, or messenger. But Jesus points to Himself, because He alone is the destination.

That is why the gospel must be preached to every creature — because only Jesus saves. Acts 4:12 declares, "Neither is there salvation in any other: for there is none other name under heaven given among men, whereby we must be saved."

Interactive Q&A

Q1: Why is Jesus the only way to God?
A1: Because sin separated humanity from God, and only Jesus, through His perfect sacrifice, reconciled us to the Father.

•

Q2: Can a sincere follower of another religion still find salvation?
A2: Sincerity without truth cannot save. Many may be sincere but sincerely wrong. Jesus is the only Savior appointed by God.

•

Q3: What makes Jesus' claim unique compared to other religious leaders?
A3: Jesus doesn't point to teachings or ideas; He points to Himself. He alone has the authority to say, 'I am the way, the truth, and the life.'

•

Q4: How can believers experience Jesus as 'the life' daily?
A4: By abiding in Him through prayer, obedience, and the Word. His Spirit continually renews and strengthens those who remain connected to Him.

Q5: How can we share this truth with others without sounding condemning?

A5: Speak with love and compassion. Present Jesus not as a religious option but as a loving Savior who gave His life for all. Let your own transformed life be a living testimony.

Reflection Points

- Am I walking daily in the way of Christ, or have I allowed other 'ways' to distract me?
- Do I fully believe that Jesus is the only truth that leads to freedom?
- Is the life of Christ actively flowing in me, producing peace, joy, and holiness?
- How can I confidently share this message of salvation with those who do not yet believe?
- What personal areas still need to submit to the truth and authority of Jesus Christ?

Closing Prayer

Lord Jesus, I thank You because You are the Way, the Truth, and the Life. No one else compares to You. I acknowledge that without You, I am lost, blind, and lifeless. Teach me to walk daily in Your way, to be guided by Your truth, and to live through Your life. Let my words, thoughts, and actions always point others to You. Fill me with boldness to proclaim that You alone are the way to the Father. May Your life in me shine brightly in a world searching for direction and meaning. I receive Your grace to walk this path faithfully until I see You face to face. In Your mighty Name, Jesus Christ, I pray — Amen.

Chapter 40

Anger – Enemy at the Edge of Breakthrough

(Ephesians 4:26–27)

"Be ye angry, and sin not: let not the sun go down upon your wrath: Neither give place to the devil." (Ephesians 4:26–27 KJV)

Introduction

Anger is one of the most misunderstood human emotions. Many Christians think all anger is sinful, but Scripture does not say that. Instead, we are commanded: "Be ye angry, and sin not." God created anger as a natural emotion

— but like fire, when uncontrolled, it can consume everything in its path.

Holy anger can bring correction, inspire positive change, and defend righteousness. Evil anger, on the other hand, is destructive, demonic, and often shows up right at the edge of breakthrough to stop progress.

Anger is not always the problem; the problem is how we respond to it.

Two Faces of Anger

1. Holy Anger (Godly Anger)

- Holy anger confronts evil and injustice with righteous zeal.
- Jesus expressed this when He drove money changers out of the temple, declaring: "My house shall be called the house of prayer" (Matthew 21:12–13).
- God Himself shows holy anger to correct rebellion and restore His people (Numbers 12:9; Psalm 7:11).
- This kind of anger is purposeful, temporary, and always aims for good.

2. Evil Anger (Sinful Anger)

- Evil anger arises from pride, selfishness, bitterness, and offense.
- Cain's anger at Abel led to the first murder (Genesis 4:6–8).
- This anger clouds judgment, escalates quickly, and destroys

relationships, families, careers, and destinies.
- Moses' uncontrolled anger at striking the rock (Numbers 20:10–12) kept him from the Promised Land.

The difference between the two is not in the feeling but in the outcome. Holy anger restores; evil anger destroys.

Signs of Demonized Anger

Anger can move beyond emotion and become a demonic stronghold. Some warning signs include:
1. Constantly angry at everything and everyone.
2. Quick-tempered and explosive over small issues.
3. Holding grudges and refusing to let go.
4. Escalating issues instead of resolving them.
5. Harbouring unforgiveness and bitterness.
6. Anger leading to hatred, malice, or violence.

Unresolved anger opens the door for Satan — "Neither give place to the devil" (Ephesians 4:27).

The Danger of Evil Anger

The Bible warns strongly against sinful anger:
• "Let all bitterness, and wrath, and anger… be put away from you" (Ephesians 4:31).
• "But now ye also put off all these; anger, wrath, malice…" (Colossians 3:8).

- "He that is soon angry dealeth foolishly" (Proverbs 14:17).
- "Make no friendship with an angry man" (Proverbs 22:24).
- "An angry man stirreth up strife" (Proverbs 29:22).

Unchecked anger can destroy marriages, careers, churches, and spiritual growth. It is truly an enemy at the edge of breakthrough — many lose opportunities not because they lack talent, but because they failed to control anger.

Overcoming Evil Anger

Here are biblical steps to break free:
1. Be Born Again – Only a new heart in Christ can overcome the old nature of wrath.
2. Be Filled with the Holy Spirit – The Spirit produces self-control (Galatians 5:22–23).
3. Renew Your Mind with the Word – Scripture trains the heart to respond with wisdom, not rage.
4. Pray Always – Prayer invites God's peace to guard our hearts (Philippians 4:6–7).
5. Practice Self-Discipline – Choose to pause, reflect, and act with restraint (James 1:19).

Interactive Q&A

Q1: Is anger always bad?
A1: No. Holy anger against sin and injustice is good. Evil

anger rooted in pride, offense, or bitterness is sinful.

Q2: What are the two categories of anger?
A2: Holy (righteous) anger, which corrects and restores; and evil (sinful) anger, which destroys.

Q3: What are the signs of demonized anger?
A3: Constant anger, quick temper, grudges, unresolved conflicts, unforgiveness, and hatred.

Q4: What dangers does the Bible warn about anger?
A4: It causes foolishness, strife, sin, broken relationships, and even loss of destiny (Ephesians 4:31; Proverbs 14:17).

Q5: How can we overcome sinful anger?
A5: Through salvation, the Holy Spirit, God's Word, prayer, and self-control.

Reflection Points

- Do I use anger to solve problems or to escalate them?
- Am I holding onto bitterness that should have ended before sunset?
- Has anger robbed me of opportunities or relationships?
- Do I see signs of demonized anger in my life?
- Am I willing to surrender my emotions fully to the control of the Holy Spirit?

Closing Prayer

Lord, thank You for teaching me that not all anger is sinful. Help me to walk in holy anger that confronts evil, but deliver me from destructive anger that ruins lives. Fill me with Your Spirit so that I may exercise self-control, resolve issues quickly, and never give place to the devil. Let my life be marked by peace, wisdom, and godly responses. In Jesus' name, Amen.

Chapter 41

Self-Esteem — Knowing Your Worth in Christ

(Revelation 19:16; 1 Peter 2:9)

"And he hath on his vesture and on his thigh a name written, KING OF KINGS, AND LORD OF LORDS." (Revelation 19:16)
"But ye are a chosen generation, a royal priesthood, an holy nation, a peculiar people; that ye should shew forth the praises of Him who hath called you out of darkness into His marvellous light." (1 Peter 2:9)

Introduction

Self-esteem is one of the most important yet misunderstood aspects of Christian living. Many people confuse self-esteem with pride, but they are very different. Pride is self-exaltation without God; self-esteem is confidence because of God. Self-esteem means self-worth — seeing yourself as valuable, capable, and loved, not because of what you have done, but because of what God says about you. It is the confidence to stand in your God-given identity and purpose.

Understanding True Self-Esteem

Self-esteem is not arrogance. You can be proud and still have low self-esteem. You can also be humble yet carry godly confidence. Pride looks down on others; true self-esteem looks up to God. Many people struggle with self-esteem when starting something new — a job, ministry, relationship, or dream. They doubt themselves, saying, "I'm not good enough." But Philippians 4:13 reminds us: "I can do all things through Christ which strengtheneth me."

The Kingdom of Kings

The Kingdom of God is unlike any other — it is a kingdom where the subjects are also kings. Yet many believers live below their royal identity. Solomon described this as a tragedy: "I have seen servants upon horses, and princes walking as servants upon the earth." (Ecclesiastes 10:7).

What Causes Low Self-Esteem?

1. History and Past Mistakes – People allow their past failures or painful experiences to define them.
2. Environment – Negative family, friends, or community influences can shape a poor self-image.
3. Words – Hurtful words spoken over your life can create deep scars if not rejected.
4. Race or Background – Some believe their color, tribe, or nationality limits them — this is a lie from the devil.
5. Lack of Motivation – Without encouragement or inspiration, people lose confidence.
6. Weak Faith – Not believing what God says about you leads to self-doubt.
7. Lack of Value-Building – You must invest in yourself — education, skill, discipline, and wisdom build confidence.
8. Negative Mindset – Many simply conclude, "I can't," and therefore never even try.

How to Overcome Low Self-Esteem

1. Renew Your Mind with God's Word — Replace every negative thought with the truth of Scripture. You are chosen, royal, holy, and peculiar (1 Peter 2:9).
2. Erase Negative History and Words — Refuse to live by your past mistakes or by what others said about you.
3. Surround Yourself with the Right Environment — Stay close to positive, faith-filled people who lift you up and remind you of your worth.
4. Feed on Motivational and Faith-Building Resources — Read, listen, and meditate on God's Word daily.
5. Develop Yourself — Learn, grow, and add value to yourself. A confident person is someone who knows they have something to offer.
6. Build Strong Faith in God — Believe that with God, all things are possible (Matthew 19:26).
7. Adopt the Mind of Christ — "Let this mind be in you, which was also in Christ Jesus." (Philippians 2:5).

Christ-Centered Confidence

Godly self-esteem is not about thinking too highly of yourself — it's about thinking rightly of yourself in Christ. You are fearfully and wonderfully made (Psalm 139:14). When you see yourself as God sees you, fear disappears, shame melts away, and courage rises.

Interactive Q&A

Q1: What is self-esteem in a Christian context?
A1: It is confidence in one's God-given worth, abilities, and purpose — not pride, but assurance of identity in Christ.

Q2: How is self-esteem different from pride?
A2: Pride exalts self apart from God; self-esteem honours God by accepting who He made you to be.

Q3: What are common causes of low self-esteem?
A3: Negative past, hurtful words, poor environment, unbelief, lack of self-development, and wrong mindset.

Q4: How can a Christian overcome low self-esteem?
A4: By renewing the mind through Scripture, building faith, developing skills, and surrounding oneself with the right people.

Q5: What mindset should a Christian have?
A5: A positive, faith-filled mindset that reflects Christ's humility and confidence — "I can do all things through Christ."

Reflection Points

- Do I see myself the way God sees me — chosen, royal, and loved?

- What negative voices or experiences have shaped how I view myself?

- Am I building my worth on God's Word or on people's opinions?

- What practical step can I take today to improve my self-worth in Christ?

- How can I help others discover their value in God?

Closing Prayer

Father, thank You for creating me in Your image and calling me Your child. Deliver me from every form of fear, shame, and inferiority. Renew my mind with Your truth. Help me to see myself the way You see me — royal, chosen, and loved. Let me walk boldly in my calling, reflect Your glory, and inspire others to find their worth in You. In Jesus' name, Amen.

Chapter 42

The Authenticity and Infallibility of God's Word

(John 10:35; Psalm 119:89; Matthew 24:35)

"Scripture cannot be broken." (John 10:35)
"Forever, O LORD, Your word is settled in heaven." (Psalm 119:89)
"Heaven and earth will pass away, but My words will never pass away." (Matthew 24:35)

Introduction

Every generation faces the question: Can the Bible be trusted? For some, it is merely an ancient book filled with religious ideas; for others, it is the living, eternal Word of God.

Scripture itself boldly declares that it is divine, unchanging, and incapable of error.

If the Bible were unreliable, Christianity would crumble — because faith, salvation, and truth all rest on God's Word. But if Scripture is indeed authentic and infallible, then believers stand on an unshakable foundation — one that endures through doubt, persecution, and time.

In this chapter, we explore why the Bible is not just historically remarkable but spiritually unbreakable — the inspired Word of God, proven true by history, prophecy, and divine preservation.

Key Concepts: Authenticity, Infallibility, and Inerrancy

Authenticity — The quality of being genuine and trustworthy.

Infallibility — The inability to fail in accomplishing its divine purpose or leading people astray.

Inerrancy — The belief that Scripture, in its original form, is completely without error in all it affirms.

Though theologians sometimes distinguish between these terms, in practice they work together. Because Scripture is "God-breathed" (2 Timothy 3:16), and God Himself cannot lie or make mistakes, His Word carries His own perfection — it is pure, reliable, and eternally true.

Evidence for the Bible's Authenticity and Infallibility

1. Survival Through Time — The Bible has endured thousands of years of opposition — burned by emperors, banned by rulers, criticized by scholars — yet it still stands as the world's most translated and distributed book.

2. Written Over Centuries, Yet One Message — From Moses to John, the Bible was written over 1,400 years by more than 35 authors — kings, prophets, shepherds, scholars, and fishermen — across three continents. Despite this diversity, it tells one coherent story: God's plan of redemption through Jesus Christ.

3. Fulfilled Prophecy — The Bible contains hundreds of prophecies, many already fulfilled with precision. The fall of Babylon, the destruction of Jerusalem, and the birth and death of Christ are historically verifiable.

4. Confirmed by History, Archaeology, and Science — Archaeological discoveries continue to validate Scripture. Critics have tried to disprove it, but findings repeatedly confirm its accuracy.

The Bible's Own Witness to Its Infallibility

Jesus declared, "Scripture cannot be broken" (John 10:35). The psalmist affirmed, "Forever, O LORD, Your word is settled in heaven" (Psalm 119:89). And Jesus again promised, "Heaven and earth will pass away, but My words will never pass away" (Matthew 24:35).

Why We Can Trust God's Word

God's nature is perfect and unchanging; His Word mirrors His character. Because Scripture is inspired by the One who cannot lie, it cannot lead astray or fail in its purpose. External evidence (archaeology, prophecy, preservation) aligns with the inner witness of the Holy Spirit, giving us full confidence in its truth.

Living in Light of an Infallible Word

- Confidence in Spiritual Decisions — When Jesus speaks, His promises stand forever.
- Authority in Doctrine and Ethics — The Bible, not culture or opinion, is our final standard.
- Strength in Times of Doubt — When life shakes, Scripture remains steady.
- Boldness in Witness — Share God's Word not as myth, but as eternal truth.

Interactive Q&A

Q1: What does it mean that Scripture is infallible?
A1: It means God's Word cannot fail or mislead; it is fully reliable in all it teaches.

Q2: Is there a difference between infallibility and inerrancy?
A2: Yes. Infallibility means the Bible will not fail in its divine purpose; inerrancy means it contains no errors in its original text.

Q3: What evidence supports the Bible's authenticity?
A3: Its endurance, unified message, fulfilled prophecy, and historical confirmation.

Q4: Do believers rely only on evidence to trust Scripture?
A4: No. The Holy Spirit confirms the truth of Scripture beyond external proof.

Q5: How should we respond to doubt about God's Word?
A5: Return to Scripture, pray for discernment, study with faith, and trust God's unchanging character.

Reflection Points

- Do I truly see the Bible as divine truth, not just literature?
- When I doubt, do I seek reassurance in God's Word or in human reasoning?
- Which prophecies or discoveries confirm my faith in Scripture's truth?

- Am I living daily according to what the Word teaches?
- How can I help others recognize the Bible's authenticity and reliability?

Closing Prayer

Heavenly Father, thank You for giving us Your eternal Word — pure, powerful, and unbreakable. Forgive us when we doubt or neglect it. Strengthen our faith in Your truth. Help us to study it, live by it, and proclaim it boldly. Let Your Spirit continually remind us that Your Word stands forever. In Jesus' name, Amen.

Chapter 43

Time Management

(Ecclesiastes 3:1)

"To everything there is a season, and a time to every purpose under the heaven."
(Ecclesiastes 3:1 KJV)

Introduction

Time is the most precious resource given to humanity — a divine gift that defines the boundaries of life itself. Every second that passes is a portion of life spent, never to be reclaimed. You can recover lost money, property, or status, but no one has ever recovered lost time. When a man is dying, his greatest desire is not riches but more time. That alone tells us how valuable time truly is. Life itself is measured in time — when time ends, life ends. The difference between the wise and the foolish, the successful and the unsuccessful, is often how they use their time.

God Himself works within time. He appoints 'a time of life' (Genesis 18:14) and 'a time appointed' for every event under heaven. He designed creation to operate in cycles — day and night, seedtime and harvest, summer and winter (Genesis 8:22). Every purpose unfolds in its season. Recognizing and respecting these divine timings is the essence of time management.

Understanding Time Management

To manage time means to discipline yourself to use it purposefully, productively, and wisely. Time management is not only about scheduling but also about discerning seasons — knowing when to act, when to wait, when to plant, and when to reap. 'There is a time to be born, and a time to die... a time to plant, and a time to pluck up that which is planted.' (Ecclesiastes 3:2). When you miss your time, you may delay or even lose your destiny.

Three Dimensions of Time Management

1. Short-Term Time Management — Managing seconds, minutes, hours, and daily routines.

2. Mid-Term Time Management — Managing weeks and months with goals and preparation.

3. Long-Term Time Management — Managing years and life stages, planning for destiny and eternity.

Reasons for Time Wastage

1. Laziness (Proverbs 19:15)

2. Procrastination — 'I will do it later' is the most dangerous phrase.

3. Bad Habits and Attitudes — drinking, gossip, oversleeping, lateness.

4. Wrong Associations — time-wasting friendships.

5. Demonic Distractions (John 10:10; Joel 2:25).

6. Uncontrollable Circumstances — illness, tragedy, war (Psalm 137:2).

How to Avoid Time Wastage

1. Plan and Document — Write down your goals and activities.

2. Discipline and Self-Control — Stay focused and avoid distractions.

3. Be Time-Conscious — Treat every hour as a divine opportunity.

4. Choose Relationships Wisely — Keep company with purposeful people (Proverbs 13:20).

5. Eliminate Bad Habits — Replace laziness and procrastination with diligence.

6. Prayer and Obedience to God's Word — Let Him direct your timing (Proverbs 16:3).

God's View of Time

God never wastes time. He created it, governs it, and uses it perfectly — the sun rises, the moon sets, and seasons follow their order. 'Summer and winter, day and night, shall not cease' (Genesis 8:22). Jesus came 'in the fullness of time' (Galatians 4:4). Likewise, your destiny unfolds in divine timing. Mismanagement of time can delay your purpose, so God expects His children to value time.

Your Attitude Toward Time

As a Christian, your time belongs to God. Each day is a divine opportunity to serve, grow, and make impact. Time is wealth, a treasure, and an investment. Once wasted, it cannot be retrieved. Treat every day as a divine deposit and every moment as sacred. 'So teach us to number our days, that we may apply our hearts unto wisdom.' (Psalm 90:12)

Interactive Q&A

Q1: What is time management, and why is it important?
A1: It means using time wisely to fulfill divine purpose.

Q2: What are the three types of time management?
A2: Short-term, mid-term, and long-term.

Q3: What are common reasons for wasting time?
A3: Laziness, procrastination, bad habits, and distractions.

Q4: How can we manage time effectively?
A4: Through planning, discipline, focus, and prayer.

Q5: What is God's attitude toward time?
A5: God values time and expects us to use it wisely for His glory.

Reflection Points

- How do I spend my daily hours?
- What activities in my life waste the most time?
- Do I treat time as a divine gift or as something casual?
- Have I identified my appointed times and seasons?
- What changes can I make today to manage time better?

Closing Prayer

Heavenly Father, thank You for the gift of time. Forgive me for the moments I have wasted. Teach me to value every second You give and to use it wisely for Your purpose. Help me to be disciplined, focused, and led by Your Spirit in all I do. May my time glorify You and advance Your kingdom. In Jesus' name, Amen.

Chapter 44

Thinking Positively Out of the Box
(Proverbs 25:2)

"It is the glory of God to conceal a thing: but the honour of kings is to search out a matter" (Proverbs 25:2).

Introduction

God delights in hiding treasures of wisdom, ideas, and opportunities in unexpected places. Proverbs 25:2 reveals a divine principle: while God conceals mysteries, it is the glory, duty, and honour of kings to search them out. True discovery comes from deep thinking — from venturing beyond the ordinary. Thinking positively and creatively out of the box is not only a success strategy; it is a biblical one.

The Glory of Searching Out a Matter

God hides treasures to be discovered by those willing to dig deeper. Gold, oil, and diamonds are not found on the surface. They are hidden in the ground, waiting for explorers with vision and determination. In the same way, divine ideas, wisdom, and solutions are often concealed, waiting for those who think beyond the ordinary to uncover them.

The honour of kings is not just in their crowns but in their ability to find answers others overlook. Every invention, breakthrough, and advancement began with someone daring to think differently. God rewards those who search diligently for answers — whether spiritual, intellectual, or practical.

Thinking Out of the Box

To think out of the box means to look beyond the usual and challenge the normal patterns of thought. It is about asking questions others ignore and daring to try what others fear. Ordinary people stay within the box, but kings, leaders, and innovators step beyond it. The beginning of the solution to any problem is thinking differently.

Consider the inventors, visionaries, and pioneers who changed the world — they refused to accept limits. They asked better questions, imagined new possibilities, and acted boldly. Even in Scripture, we see Jesus instructing Peter to launch into the deep (Luke 5:4). Shallow waters yield small catches, but deep thinking and deep faith produce abundance.

The Power of Positive Thinking

Positive thinking aligns with faith. Faith believes in possibilities even when the situation looks impossible. God does not bless negative thinking because doubt and fear contradict His nature. When you think positively, you align your mind with the creative power of God, who calls things that are not as though they were (Romans 4:17).

Abraham walked through the land God promised him, and God said, 'All the land you see, I will give to you.' (Genesis 13:17). The limit was not God's promise but Abraham's vision. The size of your thinking determines the size of your blessing.

Biblical Lessons on Thinking Beyond Limits

In 2 Kings 13:18–19, the prophet Elisha was angry because the king struck the ground only three times with arrows instead of five or six. The king's small thinking limited his victory. Many believers today also limit themselves by thinking too small, dreaming too little, or doubting God's power. God is not limited; it is our thinking that limits what He can do through us.

Isaiah 55:8–9 reminds us that God's thoughts are higher than ours. The more we align our thinking with His Word, the more we expand beyond earthly limitations.

How to Develop Out-of-the-Box Thinking

1. Renew your mind daily with the Word of God (Romans 12:2).

2. Pray for divine insight and revelation (Ephesians 1:17–18).

3. Challenge conventional assumptions and traditions.

4. Surround yourself with visionary and faith-driven people.

5. Step out in faith and take inspired risks.

6. Learn continuously and expose yourself to new ideas and experiences.

Interactive Q&A

Q1: How do you think out of the box?
A1: By refusing to accept limits, asking new questions, and thinking beyond what is usual or expected.

Q2: What is the beginning of the solution to any problem?
A2: The beginning of every solution is to think differently — out of the box.

Q3: What makes a difference between ordinary people and great achievers?
A3: Their mindset — great achievers think deeper, broader, and with faith.

Q4: What role does faith play in thinking positively?
A4: Faith gives confidence to believe in possibilities even when circumstances look impossible.

Q5: How does God reward those who search out matters?
A5: He honours them with wisdom, breakthroughs, and influence — turning them into kings and leaders.

Reflection Points

- Do I limit God's work in my life by thinking too small?
- Am I afraid to challenge the norm and pursue divine ideas?
- How often do I take time to think deeply and creatively?
- What 'deep waters' is God calling me to launch into?
- How can I use my creativity to glorify God and serve others?

Closing Prayer

Lord, thank You for giving me the mind of Christ and the ability to think beyond limitations. Help me to search out divine wisdom and to approach life's challenges with faith, creativity, and courage. Deliver me from fear, doubt, and shallow thinking. Inspire me to think positively and act boldly so that I may fulfil my destiny and glorify You in all I do. In Jesus' name, Amen.

Chapter 45

Breaking the Spirit of Poverty

(2 Corinthians 8:9; Deuteronomy 8:18; Proverbs 10:22)

"For ye know the grace of our Lord Jesus Christ, that, though He was rich, yet for your sakes He became poor, that ye through His poverty might be rich." (2 Corinthians 8:9)

Introduction

Poverty is not merely a lack of money — it is a mindset, a condition of the soul, and in many cases, a spiritual yoke that hinders progress. It robs people of vision, faith, and confidence in God's provision. Many see poverty as holiness, but the Bible never called lack a virtue. Instead, Scripture presents poverty as a curse that Christ came to redeem us from. From the Garden of Eden, man was created to live in abundance and stewardship. Adam lacked nothing; everything he needed was within reach. Poverty entered the world when sin separated man from divine supply. But in Christ, that curse has been broken. The Cross is not only for salvation from sin — it's for redemption from every curse, including the curse of poverty. The purpose of abundance is not luxury, but capacity — the ability to do God's will without limitation. God's plan is for His people to prosper with purpose.

Understanding the Spirit of Poverty

The spirit of poverty is a demonic stronghold that affects how a person thinks, feels, and acts toward resources. It deceives people into fear and limitation. It keeps them focused on survival instead of purpose. A person can have money and still be poor in mindset — worrying, doubting, and living without vision. Poverty begins where gratitude ends. It is first a spirit, then a system, and finally a cycle — one that must be broken through faith, prayer, diligence, and divine wisdom.

It manifests through:

• Fear of insufficiency — the thought that 'I will never have enough.'

• Mindset of limitation — always expecting the worst, doubting every opportunity.

- Laziness and idleness — waiting for miracles without effort. God blesses work, not wishful thinking.

- Wastefulness — squandering resources without discipline.

- Unbelief — doubting that God still blesses His people today.

God's Covenant of Prosperity

Poverty is not part of God's covenant. Prosperity — in its truest, biblical sense — is. From Genesis to Revelation, God continually establishes His covenant of provision and fruitfulness. Abraham was rich in cattle, silver, and gold (Genesis 13:2). Isaac sowed in famine and reaped a hundredfold (Genesis 26:12). Joseph prospered even in slavery (Genesis 39:2–4). David and Solomon reigned in wealth and divine favour. Deuteronomy 8:18 declares, 'It is He that giveth thee power to get wealth.' This means wealth is not only a blessing — it is divine empowerment with a covenant purpose. Godly prosperity is not selfish accumulation; it is kingdom distribution. We are blessed to be a blessing.

How to Break the Spirit of Poverty

- Renew Your Mind — Fill your thoughts with the truth of God's Word. What you believe determines what you receive (Romans 12:2).

• Walk in Obedience — God's blessings are tied to obedience. Poverty thrives in rebellion; prosperity follows submission (Isaiah 1:19).

• Be Diligent and Productive — 'The hand of the diligent maketh rich' (Proverbs 10:4). Laziness is a seed of poverty.

• Honour God with Your Substance — Giving breaks greed and fear. Tithing and generosity unlock increase (Proverbs 3:9–10).

• Reject Fear and Believe God's Promise — Fear of tomorrow keeps people small. Faith releases creativity and courage.

• Associate with Faith-Minded People — Surround yourself with people who inspire vision and growth.

• Walk in Gratitude — Gratitude is the key to multiplication. Jesus gave thanks before feeding the 5,000 (John 6:11).

Practical Truths to Remember

• Poverty is not God's plan; prosperity with purpose is.
• Wealth is not evil when it glorifies God.
• Prosperity is not about possession, but purpose.
• True riches are both material and spiritual.
• Jesus took our poverty upon Himself that we might walk in fullness and freedom.

Interactive Q&A

Q1: Is poverty the same as humility?
A1: No. Poverty limits, but humility empowers. True humility acknowledges that all increase comes from God and uses it to serve Him.

Q2: Does God want every believer to be rich?
A2: God desires every believer to prosper according to His purpose — to have sufficiency in all things and abound in every good work (2 Corinthians 9:8).

Q3: What's the difference between riches and the blessing of the Lord?
A3: Riches can come from any source, but the blessing of the Lord brings wealth with peace, joy, and purpose (Proverbs 10:22).

Q4: How can someone know they are under the spirit of poverty?
A4: When fear of giving, chronic worry, or feelings of unworthiness dominate the heart. When opportunities come, but fear says, 'It's not for me.'

Q5: What steps can help achieve financial freedom in Christ?
A5: Renew your mind, obey God's Word, be diligent, give generously, and maintain gratitude. Financial freedom starts with spiritual transformation.

Reflection Points

- Have I confused humility with poverty?
- Do I believe God truly wants me to prosper?
- What wrong beliefs have I carried about money and abundance?
- Have I been faithful with the resources I already have?
- How can I use my blessings to advance the Kingdom of God?

Closing Prayer

Heavenly Father, thank You for sending Jesus to break every curse — including the curse of poverty. I renounce every mindset of fear, limitation, and insufficiency. Fill me with divine wisdom to create, multiply, and steward Your blessings. Teach me to be diligent and generous. Let my prosperity glorify You and bless others. I receive the grace to walk in covenant abundance — with peace, purpose, and joy. In Jesus' name, Amen.

Chapter 46

Relationship at Home
(Ephesians 5:22–33; Ephesians 6:1–4)

"Wives, submit yourselves unto your own husbands, as unto the Lord. Husbands, love your wives, even as Christ also loved the church, and gave himself for it"
(Ephesians 5:22, 25)

Introduction

The home is the first community ever created by God. Before there was a church, a city, or a nation, there was a family. The strength of every society begins with the strength of the home. A home filled with love, peace, and godly relationships produces a stable and healthy society, but a home filled with strife and disunity creates confusion that spreads beyond its walls.

How you relate with your family members says much about your relationship with God. It is in the home that we first learn patience, forgiveness, humility, and love. A daughter first learns how to respect and love her future husband by how she relates to her father. A son first learns how to value and treat his future wife by how he honours his mother.

The Bible commands us to "Follow peace with all men, and holiness, without which no man shall see the Lord" (Hebrews 12:14). If peace cannot begin at home, it cannot truly exist outside it.

The Foundation of a Healthy Home

Every healthy home must be built on godly principles. Without God at its center, a home will always struggle to stand firm when trials come. The psalmist declares, *"If the foundations be destroyed, what can the righteous do?"* (Psalm 11:3), and Jesus reminds us, *"Every house divided against itself shall not stand"* (Luke 11:17).

Therefore, God must be the solid foundation upon which every family is built. When His Word and presence govern the home, peace, love, and order naturally follow.

A peaceful and loving relationship within the home is sustained by God as the foundation and strengthened through essential virtues such as:

1. Love – The foundation of all godly relationships.
2. Respect – Recognizing and valuing others' worth.
3. Honour – Showing esteem for parents, spouse, and children.
4. Understanding – Taking time to listen and empathize.
5. Trust – The glue that keeps families together.
6. Truth – Building honesty and transparency.
7. Unity – Walking together in one purpose.
8. Patience – Enduring each other's weaknesses in love.
9. Forgiveness – Letting go of past hurts to preserve peace.
10. Tolerance – Accepting differences without resentment.
11. Wisdom – Acting in discernment and gentleness.
12. Humility – Serving one another with a meek heart.

When these twelve virtues are practiced daily, the home becomes a haven of peace, and the presence of God dwells there.

Husband and Wife Relationship

Marriage is not a competition but a covenant. It is a divine partnership designed to reflect the relationship between Christ and His Church.

The Bible gives two key commandments for husbands and wives:

1. "Wives, submit yourselves unto your own husbands, as unto the Lord." *(Ephesians 5:22)*
2. "Husbands, love your wives, even as Christ also loved the church, and gave himself for it." *(Ephesians 5:25)*

Both are unconditional commands. The wife is called to submit not because her husband is perfect, but as an act of obedience to God. Submission means honour, cooperation, and respect — not inferiority.

The husband is commanded to love as Christ loves — sacrificially, faithfully, and unconditionally. True love goes beyond emotion; it gives, protects, and forgives.

Whenever love or submission is missing, the home becomes vulnerable to strife. The husband who loves will naturally lead with humility, and the wife who submits will naturally support with peace. Together they create a home where Christ is Lord.

Parents and Children Relationship

Ephesians 6:1–4 teaches balance in the relationship between parents and children.

"Children, obey your parents in the Lord: for this is right. Honour thy father and mother; which is the first commandment with promise."

Children are called to obey *in the Lord* — meaning obedience is due when it aligns with God's Word. If a parent instructs a child to do something sinful or contrary to Scripture, obedience in that case would dishonour God.

Honour, however, is lifelong. Even when children grow up and have their own homes, honouring parents continues through respect, care, and gratitude.

The promise attached to this commandment is significant — "that it may be well with thee, and thou mayest live long on the earth" (Ephesians 6:3).

To parents, Apostle Paul adds:

"And, ye fathers, provoke not your children to wrath: but bring them up in the nurture and admonition of the Lord."

Parents must avoid unnecessary harshness, anger, or comparison. Discipline should correct, not crush. Comparison destroys confidence; encouragement builds it.

A godly parent nurtures both faith and character, teaching children through love, prayer, and example.

Why Family Relationships Matter

- The family is the first ministry God established (Genesis 2:24).
- Peace at home is a foundation for peace in society.
- A healthy home raises emotionally and spiritually balanced children.
- A loving home becomes a witness of Christ's love to the world (John 13:35).

When a home honours God's order — husband loving, wife submitting, children obeying, and parents nurturing — heaven's peace fills the house.

Interactive Q&A

Q1: What is relationship at home?
A1: It is the bond and interaction among members of a family — husband, wife, parents, and children — guided by love, honour, and godly values.

Q2: Why is relationship at home so important?
A2: Because a peaceful home is the foundation of a peaceful society and reflects God's design for human relationships.

Q3: What are the key virtues for a strong home?
A3: Love, respect, honour, trust, forgiveness, patience, and humility.

Q4: What should be the relationship between husband and wife?
A4: The husband must love sacrificially as Christ loves the Church, and the wife must submit respectfully as unto the Lord.

Q5: How should parents and children relate?
A5: Children must obey and honour their parents in the Lord, while parents must nurture, love, and guide their children without provoking them to anger.

Reflection Points

- Am I contributing to peace or strife in my home?
- How do I express love, honour, and patience toward my family?
- Are there relationships in my home that need healing or forgiveness?
- Do I treat my spouse, children, or parents as God commands?
- How can I make my home a reflection of Christ's love?

Closing Prayer

Heavenly Father, thank You for the gift of family. Help us to build homes filled with love, peace, and understanding. Teach us to honour one another and walk in humility. Heal broken relationships and let Your Word reign in our hearts and homes. May our families reflect Your light to the world. In Jesus' name, Amen.

Chapter 47

Proof of Honour – Honouring God with Your Substance

(Proverbs 3:9; Matthew 15:8)

"Honour the LORD with thy substance, and with the firstfruits of all thine increase." — Proverbs 3:9 (KJV)
"This people draweth nigh unto me with their mouth, and honoureth me with their lips; but their heart is far from me."
(Matthew 15:8)

Introduction

True honour goes beyond words. Many people honour God with their lips, through songs, prayers, and religious expressions, yet their hearts remain distant. Jesus exposed this shallow worship in Matthew 15:8, showing that God is not moved by empty speech but by sincere devotion expressed through obedience and sacrifice.

To honour the Lord with your substance means to move from mere confession to tangible demonstration — to show, not just say, that God is first in your life. It is the proof of genuine faith and the evidence of a grateful heart.

People can easily give to others for personal benefit — to gain favour, recognition, or reward. But giving to God when no one sees, without applause or expectation, is the true test of faith and the highest expression of honour. When you honour God privately, He rewards you openly (Matthew 6:4).

What It Means to Honour God with Your Substance

To honour means to give weight, to recognize worth, and to esteem highly. To honour God with your substance means to give from what you possess — your income, resources, time, and effort — acknowledging that everything you own came from Him in the first place.

Honouring God with your substance is not just about money; it is about lordship. When God truly reigns in your life, it will reflect in how you handle what He has entrusted to you. Your giving becomes a declaration: 'Lord, You are my

Source, not my salary. You are my Provider, not my possessions.'

How We Give to God Directly

While it is good to give to people — family, friends, or those in need — Proverbs 3:9 speaks about honouring the Lord specifically. Giving to God directly happens when what we give promotes His Kingdom and advances His purpose on earth.

We honour the Lord with our substance when we:
1. Support the house of God.
2. Support ministries that preach the Gospel.
3. Support ministers who labour in God's vineyard.
4. Support evangelism and outreach efforts.
5. Support church projects and community missions.

Giving: The Key That Unlocks Blessing

Giving is not just a religious act — it is a divine principle. Jesus said, 'Give, and it shall be given unto you; good measure, pressed down, and shaken together, and running over...' (Luke 6:38). The Apostle Paul affirmed this in 2 Corinthians 9:6–8, teaching that those who sow generously will also reap generously.

King Solomon practiced this principle. In 1 Kings 3:4–5, he offered a thousand burnt offerings to the Lord, and that night, God appeared to him in a dream and said, 'Ask what I shall give thee.' Solomon's gift became his access point to divine abundance.

David also understood the spirit of honour. He said, 'I will not offer unto the LORD my God of that which doth cost me nothing.' (2 Samuel 24:24). True honour is never cheap. It must cost something — time, effort, or substance.

Why Honouring God with Our Substance Matters

1. It is an act of worship — acknowledging God as the ultimate Source.
2. It demonstrates love — for love always gives (John 3:16).
3. It is a test of faith — trusting God beyond visible resources.
4. It reflects commitment — showing that your heart is in His Kingdom.
5. It opens the door for blessing — 'And God is able to make all grace abound toward you; that ye, always having all sufficiency in all things, may abound to every good work' (2 Corinthians 9:8).

Beware of False Blessings

Proverbs 10:22 says, 'The blessing of the LORD, it maketh rich, and he addeth no sorrow with it.'

There are many who gain wealth through deceit or ungodly means — but such riches bring sorrow, fear, and loss. Only the blessing of the Lord enriches the soul as well as the hand. When your increase comes from obedience and honour, it carries peace, not pressure; joy, not guilt; contentment, not compromise.

Practical Ways to Honour God with Your Substance

1. Giving faithfully, joyfully and from gratitude (2 Corinthians 9:7).
2. Supporting missions and church projects.

The Heart of the Matter

Honouring God with your substance is not about how much you give — it's about how much of your heart is in it. God looks beyond the hand to the motive behind it. 'This people honoureth me with their lips, but their heart is far from me' (Matthew 15:8). To give without the heart is hypocrisy.

But to give with love, faith, and reverence is worship. Your giving becomes your proof of honour.

Interactive Q&A

Q1: What do 'substance' and 'firstfruits' mean in Proverbs 3:9?
A1: They refer to tangible possessions — the best portion of what we earn or receive — offered to God as an act of honour and gratitude.

Q2: What is the difference between giving to God and giving to others?
A2: Giving to people is good, but giving to God directly promotes His Kingdom and supports His work on earth.

Q3: Why is giving to God important?
A3: It honours Him, demonstrates faith, opens blessings, and strengthens our relationship with Him.

Q4: What kind of gifts please God?
A4: Gifts that cost something, given joyfully and in faith — not what we no longer need.

Q5: How is giving a proof of honour?
A5: Because it shows obedience when no one is watching, faith when resources seem small, and love that expects nothing in return.

Reflection Points

- Do I honour God only with words, or also with my substance?
- Do I give to impress people or to please God?
- What does my giving reveal about my faith and priorities?
- Do I give from what costs me something, or from what costs me nothing?
- Have I learned to give privately, sincerely, and joyfully?

Closing Prayer

Father, thank You for being my Source and Sustainer. Teach me to honour You not only with my lips but with my life and my substance. Deliver me from selfishness and fear. Let my giving be a true reflection of my love, faith, and trust in You. May my offerings glorify You and expand Your Kingdom on earth. Bless the work of my hands and let no sorrow be added to it. In Jesus' name, Amen.

Chapter 48

The Power of Praises
(Acts 16:25–26; Psalm 67:5–7; 2 Chronicles 20:21–22)

"At midnight Paul and Silas prayed, and sang praises unto God: and the prisoners heard them. And suddenly there was a great earthquake, so that the foundations of the prison were shaken: and immediately all the doors were opened, and every one's bands were loosed." (Acts 16:25–26)

Introduction

Praise is not just a song — it is a weapon. It is not merely an emotional expression; it is a spiritual force that moves heaven and shakes the earth. When a believer learns to praise God in all circumstances, that believer becomes unstoppable. Prayer brings petitions before God, but praise brings God Himself into the situation. While prayer invites His intervention, praise provokes His manifestation. No power of darkness can withstand the presence of the Almighty God that comes through genuine praise. Paul and Silas understood this secret. In the darkest hour of their imprisonment, they did not complain or question God — they praised Him. And heaven responded with an earthquake that broke their chains and set every captive free.

Understanding the Power of Praise

1. Praise Invites God's Presence — Psalm 22:3 says that God inhabits the praises of His people.

2. Praise Shifts Focus from Problem to Power — It redirects attention from fear to faith.

3. Praise Breaks Chains and Opens Doors — Praise carries explosive power to set captives free.

4. Praise Confuses the Enemy — As in 2 Chronicles 20:21-22, praise makes God fight for you.

5. Praise Releases Increase and Blessing — Psalm 67:5–6 teaches that praise unlocks divine increase.

When Should We Praise God?

1. In Good Times — Praise keeps your heart humble and grateful.

2. In Difficult Times — Praise becomes your declaration of faith.

3. At All Times — Psalm 34:1 reminds us to continually bless the Lord.

The Heart of True Praise

True praise flows from revelation, not emotion. It comes from knowing who God is, not what He gives. Praise is not performance; it is relationship. God looks at the heart behind the praise. Empty singing is noise, but heartfelt praise is incense before His throne.

Keys to Powerful Praise

1. Praise in Spirit and in Truth (John 4:23–24)

2. Praise with Understanding (Psalm 47:7)

3. Praise with Joy and Gladness (Psalm 100:2)

4. Praise in Unity (2 Chronicles 5:13)

5. Praise as Warfare (2 Chronicles 20:21)

Examples of Praise that Brought Victory

- Jehoshaphat's army praised and won without fighting (2 Chronicles 20).

- Paul and Silas praised and prison doors opened (Acts 16).

- Joshua and the Israelites shouted and Jericho's walls fell (Joshua 6).

- David praised continually and was called a man after God's heart (Psalm 34:1).

Interactive Q&A

Q1: What happens when believers praise God sincerely?
A1: God's presence fills the atmosphere, bringing freedom, joy, and breakthroughs.

Q2: How is praise different from prayer?
A2: Prayer petitions God for help; praise magnifies God for who He is — it moves from asking to adoring.

Q3: What does praise do to the enemy?
A3: It confuses and paralyzes the enemy; God Himself fights for those who praise Him.

Q4: When should believers praise God?
A4: At all times — in joy, in sorrow, in plenty, and in lack.

Q5: What are the keys to powerful praise?
A5: Sincerity, joy, understanding, unity, and faith.

Reflection Points

- Do I praise God only when things go well, or also in trials?
- What happens in my atmosphere when I start praising?
- How can I develop a lifestyle of praise?
- Is my praise based on emotion or revelation?
- What chains in my life could break if I began to praise consistently?

Closing Prayer

    Heavenly Father, thank You for teaching me the power of praise. Help me to live a life of continual thanksgiving, not moved by circumstances but rooted in faith. Let my praise invite Your presence, break every chain, and silence every enemy. Fill my heart with joy and my mouth with songs of victory. In every situation, I will praise You — for You are good and Your mercy endures forever. In Jesus' name, Amen.

Chapter 49

The Power and Purpose of Worship
(John 4:23–24; Psalm 95:6; Revelation 4:10–11)

"But the hour cometh, and now is, when the true worshippers shall worship the Father in spirit and in truth: for the Father seeketh such to worship him. God is a Spirit: and they that worship him must worship him in spirit and in truth." (John 4:23–24)

Introduction

Worship is more than music, words, or posture — it is the complete surrender of the heart to God. While praise celebrates God for what He has done, worship adores Him for who He is. You can praise loudly, but worship flows quietly from the depths of your being. Praise invites God's presence, but worship makes you one with His presence. From Genesis to Revelation, worship marks every encounter between God and His people. Abraham built altars of worship, David wrote songs of worship, the apostles prayed in worship, and in heaven, angels and elders bow continually before the throne saying, 'Thou art worthy, O Lord.' True worship is not occasional — it is a lifestyle.

What Is Worship?

The word worship comes from 'worth-ship' — to declare the worth of God. It is recognizing that He alone deserves all glory, honour, and devotion. It is the bowing of our hearts before His majesty, acknowledging His sovereignty and holiness. Worship is not limited to church gatherings; it happens anywhere a heart is fully yielded to God. Worship is adoration, submission, and intimacy with the Father. It's not something we attend; it's something we become.

The Heart of True Worship

Jesus said the Father is looking for 'true worshippers.' True worship does not depend on instruments, lights, or location — it depends on truth and spirit. True worship happens when the spirit of man connects with the Spirit of God in reverence, love, and obedience.

1. In Spirit — Worship flows from the regenerated spirit, not the flesh. It is the inner man responding to God's presence.

2. In Truth — Worship aligns with the Word of God. It is sincere, not pretended; authentic, not artificial.

The Power of Worship

1. Worship Brings Divine Presence — Worship opens the heavens and fills the atmosphere with God's glory (2 Chronicles 5:13–14).

2. Worship Transforms the Worshipper — You cannot behold God and remain the same (2 Corinthians 3:18).

3. Worship Breaks Chains and Brings Victory — Jehoshaphat's army and Paul and Silas experienced victory through worship.

4. Worship Establishes God's Throne in Your Life — Where God is worshipped, He reigns and takes charge of life's affairs.

5. Worship Aligns the Heart with Heaven — Worship shifts our perspective from earth to eternity.

Forms of Worship

- Verbal Worship — singing, praying, declaring God's greatness (Psalm 96:1–3).

- Physical Worship — kneeling, lifting hands, dancing, bowing (Psalm 134:2; Psalm 149:3).

- Lifestyle Worship — obedience, holiness, giving, serving (Romans 12:1).

- Quiet Worship — silent adoration and meditation (Habakkuk 2:20).

Barriers to True Worship

1. Sin and Disobedience — Sin separates us from God's presence (Isaiah 59:2).

2. Pride — Worship thrives in humility. God resists the proud but gives grace to the humble.

3. Distraction and Tradition — When worship becomes routine, it loses life (Matthew 15:8).

4. Unforgiveness — A bitter heart cannot host divine presence.

5. Lack of Focus — Worship demands full attention of the heart.

How to Develop a Lifestyle of Worship

1. Start Each Day in Gratitude — Begin with thanksgiving.

2. Meditate on God's Word Daily — The Word fuels revelation.

3. Keep a Pure Heart — Repent quickly and walk in forgiveness.

4. Worship Everywhere — In every place and moment.

5. Worship in Giving and Service — Every act of obedience is worship (Colossians 3:23).

The Reward of Worship

- God's presence and peace (Philippians 4:6–7)
- Joy unspeakable (Psalm 16:11)
- Spiritual renewal (Isaiah 40:31)
- Divine direction and revelation (Acts 13:2)
- Eternal intimacy with God (Revelation 7:9–12)

Interactive Q&A

Q1: What is true worship?
A1: True worship is the total surrender of the heart, offered to God in spirit and in truth.

Q2: How does worship differ from praise?
A2: Praise thanks God for His acts; worship adores Him for His nature.

Q3: What happens when we worship?
A3: God's presence manifests, lives are transformed, and heaven's power is released.

Q4: What are the barriers to true worship?
A4: Sin, pride, distraction, unforgiveness, and a divided heart.

Q5: How can I cultivate a lifestyle of worship?
A5: By living in gratitude, meditating on the Word, walking in obedience, and acknowledging God in all things.

Reflection Points

- Do I worship only on Sundays, or daily in my walk with God?
- Is my worship based on emotion or revelation?
- What needs to change in my life for my worship to be genuine?
- How does my worship influence my family and atmosphere?
- Do I still worship God when life is hard?

Closing Prayer

Father, You alone are worthy of all worship. Teach me to adore You not only with my lips but with my life. Cleanse my heart from distractions and pride. Let my worship create a dwelling place for Your glory in my life, my home, and my generation. I yield myself as a living sacrifice — holy and acceptable to You. Receive my worship, Lord, and let Your presence never depart from me. In Jesus' name, Amen.

Chapter 50

The Power of Praise and Worship Combined

(2 Chronicles 20:21–22; Acts 16:25–26; John 4:23–24)

"At midnight Paul and Silas prayed, and sang praises unto God: and the prisoners heard them. And suddenly there was a great earthquake, so that the foundations of the prison were shaken: and immediately all the doors were opened, and every one's bands were loosed." (Acts 16:25–26)

Introduction

Praise and worship are two sides of the same spiritual coin. Praise is the joyful expression of gratitude for what God has done, while worship is the reverent adoration of who God is. When praise and worship unite, heaven opens, and the impossible becomes possible. In Scripture, praise is often the doorway to worship. You praise until His presence fills the room, and when His glory comes, you bow in worship. Praise invites God; worship enthrones Him. Where praise brings freedom, worship brings transformation. Where praise opens the heavens, worship keeps them open. When believers learn to combine both — to celebrate God's deeds and adore His person — they experience the fullness of divine power.

The Difference Between Praise and Worship

Praise focuses on what God has done, while worship focuses on who God is. Praise is expressed through joy, music, and thanksgiving; worship through reverence, surrender, and intimacy. Praise lifts the spirit of man upward; worship brings the presence of God downward. Praise opens the door to God's presence; worship builds His throne in the heart. Praise can be loud and public, while worship can be quiet and personal. Praise prepares the way for worship, but worship is the highest form of communion.

Why Praise and Worship Are Powerful Together

1. They Invite and Establish God's Presence — Praise brings Him near; worship makes Him stay (Psalm 22:3; 2 Chronicles 5:13–14).

2. They Confuse the Enemy — Jehoshaphat's army praised God in battle, and God set ambushes against their enemies (2 Chronicles 20).

3. They Bring Deliverance and Break Chains — Paul and Silas praised and worshipped in prison, and the doors opened (Acts 16:25–26).

4. They Transform the Heart — Worship renews and refines; praise lifts faith and joy.

5. They Bring Divine Direction and Miracles — Worship tunes the spirit to hear God clearly (Acts 13:2).

The Power of Worship After Praise

Praise prepares the ground; worship plants the seed. Praise opens your mouth; worship opens your heart. When you move from clapping to bowing, from singing to surrender, the atmosphere shifts from rejoicing to revelation. David praised God with dancing and instruments (Psalm 150) but also worshipped with tears and silence (Psalm 63). No wonder God's presence followed him wherever he went.

How to Engage in Powerful Praise and Worship

1. Begin with Gratitude — Thank God intentionally for who He is and what He has done.

2. Sing or Speak from the Heart — Don't imitate others; express genuine adoration.

3. Use Scripture — Praise and worship rooted in God's Word carry power.

4. Add Posture — Lift hands, kneel, or dance; express outwardly what your heart feels inwardly.

5. Stay Sensitive — Move from praise into worship when the Spirit leads.

6. Be Consistent — Practice praise and worship daily, not only on Sundays.

Biblical Examples of Praise and Worship Power

• Jehoshaphat's victory — praise turned battle into blessing (2 Chronicles 20).

• Joshua's shout — praise brought down walls (Joshua 6).

• Paul and Silas' song — opened prison doors (Acts 16).

• Mary's worship — sitting at Jesus' feet (Luke 10:39–42).

• Heavenly worship — angels cry 'Holy, holy, holy' (Revelation 4:8–11).

The Benefits of a Life of Praise and Worship

- God's tangible presence (Psalm 16:11)
- Peace that passes understanding (Philippians 4:6–7)
- Joy and spiritual renewal (Isaiah 61:3)
- Victory in warfare (2 Chronicles 20:21–22)
- Clarity and direction from the Spirit (Acts 13:2)
- A heart aligned with heaven

Interactive Q&A

Q1: What is the difference between praise and worship?
A1: Praise celebrates God's works; worship adores His nature.

Q2: Why are praise and worship powerful together?
A2: Praise brings God near, and worship enthrones Him — together they manifest His glory.

Q3: What happens when believers praise and worship sincerely?
A3: Chains break, hearts are renewed, and God's presence fills the atmosphere.

Q4: Can praise and worship be done outside church?
A4: Yes. Every place a believer stands becomes holy ground when the heart is surrendered to God.

Q5: What is the highest form of worship?
A5: Obedience — living a life that honours God beyond the song and the sound.

Reflection Points

- Do I praise God only when things go well?
- Have I learned to move from praise into worship?
- How often do I create an atmosphere of worship in my home?
- What walls in my life could fall if I combined praise and worship daily?
- Does my worship reflect intimacy or routine?

Closing Prayer

Father, thank You for the gift of praise and worship. Teach me to celebrate Your greatness and adore Your holiness. Fill my heart with joy and reverence; let my lips continually offer You praise. As I worship, let every chain break, every burden lift, and every wall fall. Let my home, my church, and my life become an altar where Your presence dwells. I will praise You in every season and worship You with all my heart. In Jesus' name, Amen.

Chapter 51

The Reality of the Spiritual World

(2 Corinthians 4:18; Hebrews 11:3; John 14:2)

"While we look not at the things which are seen, but at the things which are not seen: for the things which are seen are temporal; but the things which are not seen are eternal." (2 Corinthians 4:18)

Introduction

The physical world we see is not all there is. Beyond what our eyes can behold lies a greater, deeper, and more permanent reality — the spiritual world. The Bible constantly points us to this truth: what we see is temporary, but what we cannot see is eternal.

From Genesis to Revelation, Scripture reveals that the unseen realm is the origin and ultimate destination of all things. "Through faith we understand that the worlds were framed by the word of God, so that things which are seen were not made of things which do appear" (Hebrews 11:3). Everything visible was birthed from the invisible. The spiritual is not less real — it is more real.

The Spiritual World Is the Source of the Physical

The spiritual world existed long before the earth was formed. God Himself, who is Spirit (John 4:24), spoke creation into existence. Angels, principalities, and spiritual laws were all present before Adam took his first breath. The physical world is like a reflection in a mirror — a temporary expression of eternal realities. What we see, feel, and touch are only shadows of greater truths.

Just as a baby in the womb believes the womb is the entirety of existence, humanity often believes that the physical world is all there is. But birth reveals a wider, brighter world beyond the womb. Likewise, when we pass from this life through death, it is not an end — it is a transition into a broader, more vivid reality: the spiritual world.

The Analogy of Birth and Eternity

In essence, the spiritual world is more real and lasting than the physical one we see. The physical world is temporary, much like a baby in the womb might think that the womb is the entirety of existence. Then, through the pain and process of birth, the baby enters a much larger, more expansive reality.

In the same way, when we pass from this physical life through the experience of death, it's like stepping into a whole new dimension—one that is spiritual and enduring.

And just as a newborn first opens its eyes to the light of a hospital room, we will one day open our spiritual eyes to the radiant light of eternity. There is a path of light there—centered on Jesus—that leads to everlasting life. Preparing for that reality means choosing that light now.

The Reality of the Invisible

Though unseen, the spiritual world constantly interacts with the physical.

- Angels are ministering spirits sent forth to help believers (Hebrews 1:14).

- Demons seek to influence and corrupt (Ephesians 6:12).

- The Holy Spirit convicts, comforts, and guides (John 16:8–13).

- Prayer and faith operate across the boundary of the seen and unseen.

When Elijah's servant trembled at the sight of enemy soldiers, the prophet prayed, "Lord, open his eyes that he may see." And suddenly the young man saw the mountain full of horses and chariots of fire round about Elisha (2 Kings 6:17). That's what happens when our spiritual eyes are opened — we see reality as it truly is.

The Temporary vs. the Eternal

Everything in this physical world fades — beauty, fame, wealth, and even life itself. But the spiritual world endures forever. Jesus said, "In my Father's house are many mansions... I go to prepare a place for you" (John 14:2). That heavenly home is not symbolic — it is real. Heaven is not a concept; it is a country. Hell is not a metaphor; it is a destination for those who reject God's light. The wisest decision anyone can make is to live now with eternity in view.

Living with Eternity in Mind

To live effectively in this world, you must first understand the next. Our daily choices should reflect our awareness of the unseen world:

1. Walk by faith, not by sight (2 Corinthians 5:7).

2. Set your affection on things above (Colossians 3:2).

3. Pursue holiness, for without it no man shall see the Lord (Hebrews 12:14).

4. Invest in eternal things — souls, service, and obedience to God's Word.

5. Seek Jesus, the Light, while it is still day (John 8:12).

Interactive Q&A

Q1: What is the difference between the physical and the spiritual world?
A1: The physical world is temporary and visible; the spiritual world is invisible and eternal.

Q2: How does the analogy of a baby in the womb help us understand eternity?
A2: Just as birth leads from a small, dark space to a greater, brighter world, death leads us from this temporary life to an eternal spiritual reality.

Q3: How can believers interact with the spiritual world today?
A3: Through faith, prayer, the Word of God, and the leading of the Holy Spirit.

Q4: What determines where we spend eternity?
A4: Our relationship with Jesus Christ — choosing His light and lordship now determines our eternal destination.

Q5: Why should we focus on the unseen?
A5: Because the unseen is permanent; it is the true reality that continues after this life ends.

Reflection Points

- Do I live more conscious of the physical or the spiritual world?
- How does knowing that life continues after death change the way I live today?
- Have I chosen the light of Jesus that leads to eternal life?
- Am I preparing for eternity or distracted by temporary things?
- How can I help others become aware of the reality of the unseen world?

Closing Prayer

Heavenly Father, thank You for opening my eyes to the reality of the spiritual world. Help me to live each day with eternity in view. Deliver me from the distractions of the temporary and anchor my heart in what is eternal. May I walk in the light of Jesus and prepare daily for the world to come. In Jesus' name, Amen.

Chapter 52

He Will Do It

(Matthew 14:22–33; Philippians 1:6; Psalm 34:19)

"Being confident of this very thing, that he which hath begun a good work in you will perform it until the day of Jesus Christ."
(Philippians 1:6)

Introduction

Life is filled with storms — some sudden, some prolonged. Sometimes, it feels like the waves of life are too strong and the wind too contrary. But in every storm, God remains faithful. The God who began a good work in your life will surely complete it.

Matthew 14:22–33 tells the story of Jesus walking on water — a passage often seen as a display of divine power or Peter's wavering faith. Yet, at its core, it is a revelation of divine love. It shows how far Jesus will go to reach His children in distress. It teaches us that no matter the situation, God will do it — He will show up, deliver, and perform His word in His time.

The Message Behind the Miracle

When the disciples were caught in a violent storm, the Bible says, "But the ship was now in the midst of the sea, tossed with waves: for the wind was contrary" (Matthew 14:24). They were frightened, exhausted, and hopeless. But while they struggled, Jesus was watching. Though He had stayed behind to pray, He knew exactly what was happening to them.

Jesus had many options:

1. He could have rebuked the storm from the mountain.

2. He could have borrowed a boat to meet them.

3. He could have appeared instantly in the ship.

4. But He chose to walk on the water — the very thing threatening their lives.

Why? Because He wanted to show them that what threatens to destroy you is under His feet. He wanted them to see His love in action, not from afar but up close. Jesus walked through the storm to show that He is not distant from our pain — He steps into it with us.

The God Who Comes Through

Jesus walking on water was not to prove His power but to prove His care. God will always go to any length, cross any sea, and move through any storm to rescue His people.

This same love divided the Red Sea for Israel, shut the lions' mouths for Daniel, stood with the three Hebrew boys in the fiery furnace, and raised Jesus from the grave. God's pattern is consistent — He shows up when hope seems gone, when strength is finished, and when only faith remains.

"Many are the afflictions of the righteous: but the LORD delivereth him out of them all." — Psalm 34:19

He delivers from all of them — not some, not most, but all. He might wait until the last minute, but He is never late. His timing is perfect, and His plan is sure.

When God Seems Silent

Where was God when Joseph was sold into slavery? Where was He when Pharaoh pursued Israel to the Red Sea? Where was He when Daniel faced the lions or when Jesus hung on the cross? He was there — silently orchestrating deliverance. God's silence does not mean absence. He was preparing the miracle behind the scenes.

The story of Jesus walking on water reminds us: when the night is darkest and the sea is roughest, that's often when God is closest. Sometimes, He waits for every human effort to fail so that His glory can be fully revealed.

Trust Him — He Will Do It

No matter what you are going through — sickness, delay, rejection, or loss — God has not forgotten you. His promises still stand.

"For the vision is yet for an appointed time, but at the end it shall speak, and not lie: though it tarry, wait for it; because it will surely come, it will not tarry." — Habakkuk 2:3

God's timetable may not match yours, but His word will never fail. Trust Him even when you don't see Him. Like

Peter, step out of the boat if He calls you. Even if you begin to sink, His hand is right there to lift you up again.

"He will make everything beautiful in his time" (Ecclesiastes 3:11). If God did not leave Jesus in the grave, He will not leave you in your storm. Tell yourself, "He will do it." Yes, He will.

Encouragement for Believers

When life feels like an endless storm:

- Remember that Jesus sees you.

- Remember that He cares.

- Remember that He will come through — even if it means walking on water to reach you.

Hold on to His promises. The same God who delivered Daniel, Joseph, and the disciples will deliver you too.

"My God shall supply all your need according to his riches in glory by Christ Jesus" (Philippians 4:19).

"You can do all things through Christ which strengthens you" (Philippians 4:13).

"And we know that all things work together for good to them that love God, to them who are the called according to his purpose" (Romans 8:28 KJV)

Interactive Q&A

Q1: Why does God sometimes wait until the last minute to deliver us?
A1: To strengthen our faith, teach us dependence, and display His glory when human strength is gone.

Q2: How many of the righteous' afflictions does God deliver them from?
A2: All of them — not one is left behind (Psalm 34:19).

Q3: Why did Jesus walk on water?
A3: Not to prove His power but to demonstrate His love and show His mastery over every storm.

Q4: What should a believer do when God seems silent?
A4: Trust His plan, remain faithful, and remember that silence is not absence. God is always working.

Q5: What does Philippians 1:6 assure us of?
A5: That whatever God starts in your life, He will finish. He never abandons His promises.

Reflection Points

- What does this story reveal about God's love and timing?
- When has God come through for you at the last minute?
- How can you trust Him more when you don't understand His plan?
- What storms are you facing today that you need to surrender to Him?
- How can your faith in God's timing encourage someone else?

Closing Prayer

Father, thank You for being faithful through every storm. Teach me to trust You even when I can't see the way ahead. Strengthen my heart to wait patiently for Your timing. Remind me that You are never late and that You will do what You have promised. Calm every storm in my life and help me to walk in peace, faith, and confidence. In Jesus' name, Amen.

Chapter 53

Christmas — Celebrating Christ, Not Just a Day

(Matthew 2:1–16; Luke 2:6–18)

"For unto you is born this day in the city of David a Saviour, which is Christ the Lord." — Luke 2:11 (KJV)

Introduction

Every December, the world turns its attention — even if briefly — to the name of Jesus Christ. Streets light up, families gather, and songs of joy fill the air. Yet, for many, the question remains: Is Christmas biblical? Some argue that Jesus was not born in December. Others claim that the Bible does not command us to celebrate His birth. They point out that the two birthday celebrations recorded in Scripture — Pharaoh's (Genesis 40:20–22) and Herod's (Matthew 14:6–12) — ended in tragedy. They also note that Jesus instructed us to remember His death (Luke 22:19; 1 Corinthians 11:23–26), not His birth.

While these arguments may hold some truth, they miss the heart of the matter. The celebration of Jesus' birth is indeed found in Scripture. When Christ was born, angels appeared to shepherds, saying, "Glory to God in the highest, and on earth peace, goodwill toward men" (Luke 2:14). God Himself sent messengers from heaven to announce and celebrate His Son's arrival. Wise men from the east travelled to worship Him and presented gifts. That is the essence of Christmas — celebrating Jesus. Christmas is not merely a date — it is a declaration: Christ has come!

The True Meaning of Christmas

I do not see Christmas as the "birthday" of Jesus, but as a celebration of Jesus. It is a season humanity has set aside to remember the greatest event in history — when God became man and dwelt among us (John 1:14). Easter is celebrated mainly by believers, but Christmas is a time when the entire world — knowingly or unknowingly — acknowledges Christ. It is the only season when the name of Jesus is heard in every song, every shop, and every home. If the world chooses to sing about Jesus, let us not be silent! So rather than arguing about the date, let us seize the opportunity to proclaim the truth — Christ was born, He lived, He died, and He rose again!

A Biblical Prototype of Christmas

1. It is a celebration of Jesus, not a date — The wise men didn't celebrate December; they celebrated the Christ (Matthew 2:1–2).

2. It must be centred on Jesus — Every detail in Matthew 2 revolves around Him — the star, the journey, the gifts, and the worship.

3. It should be celebrated with wisdom, not foolishness — There were many men in the east, but only the wise came to Jesus.

4. It should be a time of reflection — The wise men reflected deeply on the star and sought its meaning.

5. It should inspire commitment — The wise men travelled far, enduring hardship to find Jesus.

6. It should be a season of worship — The goal of the wise men's journey was to worship Jesus (Matthew 2:11).

7. It should be a time of visitation — The wise men visited Jesus; Christmas is a time to visit and care for others.

8. It should be filled with joy and peace — "When they saw the star, they rejoiced with exceeding great joy" (Matthew 2:10).

9. It should be marked by giving — The wise men gave gifts; when we give to others, we give to Christ (Matthew 25:40).

10. It should be a time of purity — Gold symbolized purity and divine worth.

11. It should be a time to proclaim Jesus — The wise men spoke of Jesus even before kings.

12. It should be a time of courage — The wise men were bold to acknowledge Jesus before Herod.

The Foolishness of Herod

In contrast, King Herod responded to the news of Jesus' birth with fear, anger, and violence (Matthew 2:16). He represents those who celebrate Christmas in the wrong spirit — through pride, jealousy, drunkenness, immorality, or competition. Herod's reaction cost lives. In the same way, many lose spiritual life during the Christmas season because of unwise choices. Be among the wise men, not the Herods. Celebrate with reverence, gratitude, and holiness.

How to Celebrate Christmas Wisely

- Put Christ at the centre of your celebration.
- Spend time with family in love and unity.
- Worship, reflect, and renew your relationship with God.
- Give generously to those in need.
- Avoid wastefulness, drunkenness, and comparison.
- Share the message of Christ wherever you go.

Interactive Q&A

Q1: What are some of the arguments people have about Christmas?
A1: Some argue that Jesus wasn't born in December, that birthday celebrations are not biblical, or that Jesus never commanded His birth to be celebrated.

Q2: What is Christmas truly about?
A2: It's not about the date of His birth, but about celebrating the coming of Jesus — God's greatest gift to humanity.

Q3: How can people celebrate Christmas wisely?
A3: By centring it on Jesus, practicing love and generosity, worshipping God, and avoiding worldliness.

Q4: How do some celebrate Christmas foolishly?
A4: Through drunkenness, competition, reckless spending, and immorality — losing sight of Christ.

Q5: What should Christmas be more about?
A5: It should be about worship, reflection, and proclaiming Jesus as Lord and Saviour to all.

Reflection Points

- What does Christmas mean to me personally — a holiday or a holy day?
- How can I keep Jesus at the centre of my celebration?
- In what ways can I be a "wise man" in my approach to Christmas this year?
- How can I use this season to bless and reach others for Christ?
- Do my actions reflect the joy, peace, and love that Jesus brings?

Closing Prayer

Heavenly Father, thank You for sending Jesus — the greatest gift to mankind. Help me to celebrate Christmas with wisdom, purity, and joy. May my heart and home reflect Your peace and love. Keep me from distraction and sin, and teach me to share the message of Your Son with boldness. Let this

Christmas be about You, Lord Jesus — my Saviour and King. Amen.

Chapter 54

Holy Communion — Remembering the Covenant

(Matthew 26:26–29; 1 Corinthians 11:23–26)

> *"And as they were eating, Jesus took bread, and blessed it, and brake it, and gave it to the disciples, and said, Take, eat; this is my body. And he took the cup, and gave thanks, and gave it to them, saying, Drink ye all of it; For this is my blood of the new testament, which is shed for many for the remission of sins." (Matthew 26:26–28)*

Introduction

The Holy Communion — also known as the Lord's Supper — is one of the most sacred ordinances given to the Church. It was instituted by our Lord Jesus Christ on the night He was betrayed. Through it, believers remember His sacrifice, proclaim His death, and renew their covenant with Him. The Communion is not merely a religious ritual. It is a deep spiritual experience that connects heaven and earth. Each time we partake, we affirm that we belong to Christ — body, soul, and spirit. Jesus said, "Do this in remembrance of Me" (Luke 22:19). Those words are not just an invitation; they are a command — a reminder that the foundation of our faith is what Christ accomplished on the Cross.

The Meaning of Holy Communion

The Holy Communion has three central elements — the bread, the cup, and the meaning behind them:

1. The Bread – Symbolizes the body of Christ, broken for us. It represents His suffering, His sacrifice, and the stripes He bore for our healing (Isaiah 53:5).

2. The Cup – Symbolizes the blood of Christ, shed for the forgiveness of sins. The New Covenant was sealed once and for all with the precious blood of Jesus (Hebrews 9:12).

3. The Meaning – Communion means fellowship. It is our participation in the life and victory of Jesus Christ and a reminder that we are one body in Him.

The Covenant Connection

When Jesus said, "This is My blood of the New Testament," He was declaring the birth of a new covenant — one not based on law, but on grace. Through this covenant: our sins are forgiven, our relationship with God is restored, and we gain access to the blessings of redemption. This covenant is sealed in the blood of Jesus, and every time we take the Communion, we renew that covenant. It is a sacred reminder that we belong to Him and that His promises toward us are sure.

The Power of Communion

1. It brings spiritual healing – "With His stripes we are healed" (Isaiah 53:5). Many believers experience healing through Communion because it represents wholeness in Christ.

2. It strengthens our faith – Each time we partake, we proclaim again that Jesus died, rose, and is coming again (1 Corinthians 11:26).

3. It renews unity in the body of Christ – Communion reminds us that we are one body: "For we being many are one bread, and one body" (1 Corinthians 10:17).

4. It reminds us of His soon return – Jesus said, "I will not drink henceforth of this fruit of the vine, until that day when I drink it new with you in My Father's kingdom" (Matthew 26:29).

How to Partake Worthily

The Apostle Paul gives a strong warning in 1 Corinthians 11:27–29: "Wherefore whosoever shall eat this bread, and drink this cup of the Lord, unworthily, shall be guilty of the body and blood of the Lord." To partake worthily means to examine yourself — repent of sin and unforgiveness before you partake, recognize the sacredness of the moment, and partake with reverence, gratitude, and understanding. The table of the Lord is not a place of pride but of humility — where we remember that we are saved not by works, but by grace.

What Holy Communion Reminds Us Of

1. His Sacrifice – He died that we might live.

2. His Love – He gave His life for us even while we were sinners.

3. His Promise – He is coming back again to receive His Church.

Interactive Q&A

Q1: What does the bread in Communion symbolize?
A1: The body of Christ, broken for our healing and wholeness.

Q2: What does the cup represent?
A2: The blood of Christ, shed for the forgiveness of our sins and sealing of the New Covenant.

Q3: Why is Holy Communion important?
A3: It reminds us of Christ's sacrifice, renews our covenant, strengthens our faith, and unites the Church.

Q4: What does it mean to partake unworthily?
A4: To take Communion carelessly, without repentance, reverence, or understanding of its sacred meaning.

Q5: What does Communion point us toward?
A5: The soon return of Jesus and eternal fellowship with Him in His Kingdom.

Reflection Points

- Do I truly understand the meaning of the Communion, or do I treat it as routine?
- Is my heart free of bitterness, unforgiveness, and sin before

I partake?
- When I take the bread and cup, do I remember His love with gratitude?
- Am I walking daily in the covenant I renew through Communion?

Closing Prayer

Lord Jesus, thank You for giving Your life for me. Thank You for the blood that cleanses and the body that heals. As I partake of Your table, I remember Your sacrifice, receive Your strength, and renew my covenant with You. Let this Communion draw me closer to You and deepen my love for others. Help me to live in the power of Your grace until the day I dine with You in glory. In Jesus' name, Amen.

Chapter 55

The Rapture: The Blessed Hope of Believers

(1 Thessalonians 4:13–18; 1 Corinthians 15:51–52; Matthew 24:36–44)

"For the Lord himself shall descend from heaven with a shout, with the voice of the archangel, and with the trump of God: and the dead in Christ shall rise first: Then we which are alive and remain shall be caught up together with them in the clouds, to meet the Lord in the air: and so shall we ever be with the Lord." (1 Thessalonians 4:16–17)

Introduction

The rapture is one of the most glorious promises in the Bible — the moment when Jesus Christ will return in the air to gather His saints, both the living and the dead, to Himself. The word 'rapture' comes from the Latin 'rapturo,' which means 'caught up' — the same expression used by Paul in 1 Thessalonians 4:17. For the believer, the rapture is not a theory or a myth. It is a divine reality — the blessed hope of all who love Jesus and long for His appearing (Titus 2:13). It marks the end of the Church Age and the beginning of eternity with Christ.

What Is the Rapture?

The rapture is the supernatural event where all true believers in Jesus Christ — both the living and those who have died in faith — will be instantly transformed and caught up to meet the Lord in the air. Paul explains it clearly in 1 Corinthians 15:51–52: "Behold, I show you a mystery; We shall not all sleep, but we shall all be changed, In a moment, in the twinkling of an eye, at the last trump: for the trumpet shall sound, and the dead shall be raised incorruptible, and we shall be changed."

The Purpose of the Rapture

1. To rescue the Church from the coming wrath (1 Thessalonians 1:10; Revelation 3:10).

2. To reward the faithful (2 Corinthians 5:10).

3. To unite believers with Christ forever (1 Thessalonians 4:17).

4. To fulfill God's promises (John 14:3).

The Signs of the Rapture's Nearness

1. Increase in lawlessness and moral decay (2 Timothy 3:1–5).

2. Rise of false prophets and deception (Matthew 24:11).

3. Wars, natural disasters, and global instability (Matthew 24:6–7).

4. Technology aligning with prophecy (Revelation 13:16–17).

5. The gospel being preached in all the world (Matthew 24:14).

6. The restoration of Israel (Ezekiel 37; Matthew 24:32–34).

What Will Happen During the Rapture

1. The Lord will descend from Heaven.

2. There will be a shout, a voice, and a trumpet (1 Thessalonians 4:16).

3. The dead in Christ will rise first.

4. The living believers will be transformed (1 Corinthians 15:53).

5. Together, we will meet the Lord in the air.

6. Eternal fellowship begins — 'And so shall we ever be with the Lord.'

How to Prepare for the Rapture

1. Be Born Again – Only those who belong to Christ will be taken (John 3:3).

2. Live in Holiness – 'Without holiness no man shall see the Lord' (Hebrews 12:14).

3. Walk in Love and Forgiveness – Keep no bitterness in your heart (Ephesians 4:32).

4. Stay Watchful and Prayerful – 'Watch and pray, that ye may be accounted worthy' (Luke 21:36).

5. Serve Faithfully – Let Jesus find you doing His will when He comes (Matthew 24:46).

6. Hold Fast in Faith – Don't let the trials of this world shake your hope (1 Corinthians 15:58).

Why Many Will Miss the Rapture

Jesus warned that not everyone who calls Him 'Lord' will enter the Kingdom (Matthew 7:21–23). Many will miss the rapture because they:

- Profess Christ but do not possess Him.

- Love the world more than God.

- Are spiritually asleep.

- Neglect repentance and holy living.

Encouragement for Believers

Paul concludes his teaching on the rapture with these words: 'Wherefore comfort one another with these words' (1 Thessalonians 4:18). The rapture is not to make us fearful but hopeful. It reminds us that this world is not our home. Trials, pain, and suffering will one day end. Every tear will be wiped away. Every sacrifice will be rewarded. Hold on — Jesus is coming soon!

Interactive Q&A

Q1: What is the rapture?
A1: The rapture is the catching away of believers to meet Christ in the air, as described in 1 Thessalonians 4:16–17.

Q2: How is the rapture different from the second coming?
A2: In the rapture, Jesus comes for His Church; in the second coming, He returns with His Church.

Q3: Why is the rapture important to believers?
A3: It is our blessed hope — a reminder of God's promise to rescue His people and reward their faithfulness.

Q4: How can believers prepare for the rapture?
A4: By living holy, staying watchful, walking in love, and remaining faithful to Christ.

Q5: What does the rapture teach us about God's love?
A5: It shows that God has not forgotten His people — He is coming personally to receive us to Himself.

Reflection Points

- Do I truly believe that Jesus could return at any moment?
- Am I living in readiness, or am I distracted by the world?
- What would I do differently if I knew Jesus was coming tomorrow?
- Am I helping others to prepare for His return?

- Is my heart filled with hope or fear about the coming of the Lord?

Closing Prayer

Heavenly Father, thank You for the blessed hope of the rapture. Help me to live daily in readiness for the return of Jesus. Keep my heart pure, my faith strong, and my spirit awake. May I be found faithful when the trumpet sounds. Let me not be distracted by this world but be filled with joy and expectation of Your coming. Even so, come, Lord Jesus. Amen.

Chapter 56

Holiness — The Beauty of God's Nature

(Hebrews 12:14; 1 Peter 1:15–16; Leviticus 20:7–8; Matthew 5:8)

"Follow peace with all men, and holiness, without which no man shall see the Lord." (Hebrews 12:14)
"But as he which hath called you is holy, so be ye holy in all manner of conversation; Because it is written, Be ye holy; for I am holy." (1 Peter 1:15–16)

Introduction

Holiness is not a suggestion — it is a command. It is the very nature of God and the true mark of every genuine believer. Holiness simply means being set apart — separated from sin, dedicated unto God, and walking in obedience to His Word. In a world that celebrates compromise, holiness distinguishes the children of God from the children of the world. It is not old-fashioned; it is eternal. God has not changed His standard. He is still saying today, "Be ye holy, for I am holy." Holiness is not just about what we do — it's about who we are. It begins in the heart and flows into our thoughts, words, and actions. It is the reflection of God's purity in the life of a man or woman fully yielded to Him.

Understanding Holiness

The word 'holy' comes from the Hebrew word 'qadosh', meaning "to be separated" or "set apart." God Himself is holy — pure, undefiled, perfect in all His ways. His holiness is His glory revealed, and it is the standard by which everything else is measured.

To be holy, therefore, means:

- To be separated from sin.

- To live in moral purity and righteousness.

- To be consecrated — fully devoted to God.

Holiness is not about rules and restrictions; it is about relationship. When you love God deeply, you will desire to please Him completely.

Why Holiness Matters

1. It Reflects God's Character — God is holy, and as His children, we must carry His likeness (1 Peter 1:15–16).

2. It Is the Key to Fellowship with God — Without holiness, no man shall see the Lord (Hebrews 12:14).

3. It Brings Power and Authority — A holy life is a powerful life. Samson lost his power when he lost his purity.

4. It Protects You from the Enemy — Sin gives Satan access; holiness shuts the door.

5. It Attracts Divine Presence — God dwells in holy places and among holy people.

The Foundation of True Holiness

1. Salvation — Holiness begins with being born again. You cannot live holy without the Holy Spirit.

2. The Word of God — 'Sanctify them through thy truth: thy word is truth' (John 17:17).

3. The Fear of the Lord — The fear of God keeps you from sinning (Proverbs 16:6).

4. Love for God — Holiness flows naturally when you love God deeply.

5. The Help of the Holy Spirit — The Spirit empowers us to live beyond the desires of the flesh (Galatians 5:16).

Practical Dimensions of Holiness

1. Holiness of Heart — Purity of motives and thoughts (Psalm 51:10).

2. Holiness of Speech — Words seasoned with grace (Ephesians 4:29).

3. Holiness of Conduct — Living righteously in public and private (Philippians 2:15).

4. Holiness in Relationships — Walking in love, forgiveness, and truth.

5. Holiness in Appearance — Modesty, simplicity, and dignity that honor God.

Enemies of Holiness

1. Compromise — Trying to please both God and the world.

2. Carnality — Living according to fleshly desires rather than the Spirit.

3. Pride — Holiness and pride cannot dwell together.

4. Neglect of the Word and Prayer — Without daily communion with God, holiness fades.

5. Bad Company — Evil communication corrupts good manners (1 Corinthians 15:33).

Rewards of Holiness

1. Closeness to God — 'Draw nigh to God, and He will draw nigh to you' (James 4:8).

2. Answered Prayers — 'The effectual fervent prayer of a righteous man availeth much' (James 5:16).

3. Peace of Mind — Holiness produces inner peace.

4. Divine Favour — God delights in the upright (Proverbs 11:20).

5. Eternal Life — The holy shall see the Lord (Revelation 21:27).

How to Walk in Holiness

1. Stay in the Word — The Word washes and renews your mind.

2. Pray Constantly — Prayer keeps you connected and sensitive to God.

3. Guard Your Heart — Avoid what defiles your spirit (Proverbs 4:23).

4. Flee Temptation — Don't fight sin; flee from it (2 Timothy 2:22).

5. Confess Quickly — If you fall, repent immediately and be restored.

6. Walk in the Spirit — Let the Holy Spirit control your desires and decisions.

Interactive Q&A

Q1: What does holiness mean?
A1: Holiness means being separated from sin and dedicated to God in purity, obedience, and love.

Q2: Can a person live holy without the Holy Spirit?
A2: No. The Holy Spirit empowers believers to overcome sin and live according to God's will.

Q3: Why is holiness important to the Christian life?
A3: Without holiness, no one can have fellowship with God or see His kingdom (Hebrews 12:14).

Q4: Is holiness about outward appearance only?
A4: No. Holiness begins in the heart and reflects outwardly through words, actions, and conduct.

Q5: What are the benefits of living a holy life?
A5: Intimacy with God, divine favor, peace, spiritual authority, and eternal life.

Reflection Points

- Do I pursue holiness out of love for God or fear of judgment?
- Are there hidden sins or compromises I need to let go of?
- Does my lifestyle reflect the holiness of the God I serve?
- What areas of my life need purification?
- How can I help others desire and walk in holiness?

Closing Prayer

Heavenly Father, You are holy and perfect in all Your ways. I thank You for calling me out of darkness into Your marvelous light. Create in me a clean heart and renew a right spirit within me. Fill me with Your Holy Spirit and help me to walk in purity, truth, and obedience. Let my life reflect Your holiness in everything I do. I choose to live for You, Lord — holy and set apart. In Jesus' name, Amen.

Chapter 57

Do Not Be Anxious About Anything
(Philippians 4:6; Matthew 6:24–34)

"Do not be anxious about anything, but in everything by prayer and supplication with thanksgiving let your requests be made known to God." (Philippians 4:6 ESV)

Introduction

Anxiety, fear, and worry are enemies of faith. They drain energy, cloud judgment, and rob believers of peace. The Word of God makes it clear — anxiety is not part of the believer's portion. The same God who feeds the birds and clothes the lilies of the field will surely take care of His own. Anxiousness is not just a human weakness; it is a spiritual distraction. It shifts focus from God's power to man's limitation. Jesus commanded us not to worry because worry accomplishes nothing. "Which of you by taking thought can add one cubit unto his stature?" (Matthew 6:27). Faith, not fear, pleases God. "Without faith it is impossible to please Him" (Hebrews 11:6).

Understanding Anxiety and Faith

To be anxious means to be weighed down with care, uncertain about the outcome, or consumed by fear of the future. Anxiety says, "What if it doesn't work?" Faith says, "Even if I don't see it yet, I believe God will do it." A believer who truly trusts God has peace even in the storm. When you hand your burdens to God, you stop carrying what He has already promised to handle. "The battle is the Lord's" (1 Samuel 17:47). Daniel, Shadrach, Meshach, and Abednego were not anxious in Babylon. Though threatened with death, they rested in God's faithfulness — and God did not fail them.

The Trap of Worry

The devil uses worry to entangle believers and weaken their confidence. Scripture warns: "Thou therefore endure hardness, as a good soldier of Jesus Christ. No man that warreth entangleth himself with the affairs of this life; that he may please Him who hath chosen him to be a soldier." (2 Timothy 2:3–4 KJV). Worry is not harmless; it is dangerous. It leads to fear, confusion, frustration, depression, and unbelief. Abraham and Sarah worried when God's promise seemed delayed and made a costly mistake by turning to Hagar (Genesis 16). Jeroboam feared losing his kingdom and built idols in Israel (1 Kings 12:25–33). Anxiety leads to impatience, and impatience leads to disobedience. There is nothing good about anxiety — it has no power to solve any problem. Instead, it steals peace, damages health, and shortens life.

Jesus' Teaching on Anxiety

Jesus devoted an entire section of His Sermon on the Mount to warn against worry (Matthew 6:24–34). He reminded us that God provides for birds and flowers — creations far less valuable than His children. If God takes care of them, He will surely take care of you. The Lord's message is simple:

• Don't worry about tomorrow; tomorrow is in God's hands.

• Seek first the Kingdom of God and His righteousness.

- Trust God's timing — everything He does is beautiful in its season (Ecclesiastes 3:11).

The Path to Freedom from Anxiety

1. Cast Your Cares on God — 'Casting all your care upon Him; for He careth for you' (1 Peter 5:7). God doesn't just tolerate your burden; He invites you to hand it over.

2. Pray About Everything — Prayer is the antidote to worry. Philippians 4:6 teaches us to replace anxiety with prayer and thanksgiving.

3. Live by Faith, Not by Sight — 'For we walk by faith, not by sight' (2 Corinthians 5:7).

4. Renew Your Mind with the Word — When you meditate on the Word, peace replaces fear (Joshua 1:8; Isaiah 26:3).

5. Keep a Grateful Heart — Thanksgiving shifts focus from what's missing to what's present. Gratitude invites peace.

6. Trust God's Sovereignty — 'The earth is the Lord's, and the fullness thereof' (Psalm 24:1). Nothing is out of His control.

When God Seems Silent

Sometimes God allows silence to strengthen our trust. Joseph was sold, imprisoned, and forgotten — yet in the end, God lifted him higher than he imagined. The same God who parted the Red Sea and shut the lions' mouths will show up for you — in His time. "Though it tarry, wait for it; because it will surely come" (Habakkuk 2:3). Your delay is not denial. God is working behind the scenes, aligning everything for your good (Romans 8:28).

Faith Declaration

- I refuse to worry about my future — God holds it.
- I choose faith over fear.
- I believe that all things are working together for my good.
- I rest in God's timing, not my own.
- I cast all my cares on Him, for He cares for me.

Interactive Q&A

Q1: What can worry and anxiety achieve in solving life's problems?

A1: Nothing. They only drain faith and peace, leading to confusion and frustration.

Q2: Are worries and anxieties sinful?
A2: Yes, because they reveal lack of trust in God's faithfulness and goodness.

Q3: What leads people into anxiety?
A3: Lack of faith, impatience, ignorance of God's Word, and focusing on circumstances rather than promises.

Q4: How can believers avoid anxiety?
A4: By praying, trusting God, staying in His Word, and casting every care upon Him.

Q5: How do people of faith handle difficult situations?
A5: They rest in God's promises, maintain peace through prayer, and wait patiently for His perfect timing.

Reflection Points

- Do I pray more than I worry?
- What fears or anxieties have I been holding instead of handing over to God?
- Do I truly believe that God is in control of every detail of my life?
- How can I replace worry with worship in daily life?
- What promises from Scripture can I meditate on during moments of fear?

Closing Prayer

Heavenly Father, thank You for being my peace in every storm. I confess that I have sometimes allowed worry to rule my mind. Forgive me, Lord. Today, I choose to trust You completely. I lay all my burdens, fears, and concerns at Your feet. Fill me with the peace that passes all understanding. Teach me to walk by faith and not by sight. I believe You will perfect all that concerns me. In Jesus' name, Amen.

Chapter 58

Idea, Goal, Planning, and Action
(Luke 14:28)

"For which of you, intending to build a tower, sitteth not down first, and counteth the cost, whether he have sufficient to finish it?" — Luke 14:28 (KJV)

Introduction

Every great accomplishment begins with an idea — but not every idea becomes reality. Many people stop at the idea stage and never move forward. Some confuse ideas with goals, and because of that, their vision never takes shape.

Jesus, in His divine wisdom, captures the full journey of success — from idea to completion — in one profound verse: Luke 14:28. This passage teaches that before building anything worthwhile, one must first think, plan, and act with wisdom.

From Idea to Goal

There is only a thin line between an idea and a goal. An idea is simply a thought or concept — something you want to do. A goal is when that idea becomes defined, measurable, and clear. "Building" is an idea. But "building a tower" is a goal. An idea without a goal is like a dream without direction. The builder in Luke 14:28 had an idea — to build — but his goal gave that idea shape and meaning. Once he decided to build a tower, everyone, including God, could understand his intention. Your idea gives birth to inspiration. Your goal gives birth to clarity.

The Importance of Planning

The next stage after setting a goal is planning. Planning means arranging a sequence of steps that will help you achieve your goal. A plan is a bridge between where you are and where you want to be. In Luke 14:28–30, Jesus warns of a man who started to build but failed to finish because he did not plan. The result? "All that behold it begin to mock him." Lack of planning leads to failure, frustration, disappointment, and mockery. The man had a good idea and a clear goal — but without a plan, he could not complete it. Someone once said, "Failing to plan is planning to fail."

Before you begin any project — whether spiritual, business, academic, or family — sit down and think through the process. Write down the steps. Pray about them. Seek advice if necessary. Jesus Himself said, "Ask, and you shall receive; seek, and you shall find" (Matthew 7:7). A plan may involve sub-goals such as saving money weekly, learning a skill, cutting unnecessary expenses, or allocating time wisely. Each step is part of the structure that leads to your final goal.

A Simple Example

Suppose your idea is to lose weight. That's good, but it's not a goal yet. Your goal might be: "I want to lose 10 kilograms." That's measurable. It gives direction. Now, what is your plan? Exercise for 10 minutes daily. Adjust your meals — type, quality, and quantity. Once you write down your plan, you can measure your progress. The builder in Luke 14:28 failed because he started without sitting down to plan. Don't make that mistake. Planning involves thinking, researching, and writing. It is a spiritual discipline as much as a mental one.

The King of Them All: Action

The final step — the most powerful of all — is action. You can have great ideas, smart goals, and brilliant plans, but if you never act, nothing happens. This is where most people fail. They think, they plan, they talk — but they never do. Action turns faith into reality. "Faith without works is dead" (James 2:26). It is better to take action and fail than to fail to take action. Start that business, ministry, book, or spiritual growth journey. Don't wait until conditions are perfect — they never will be.

Enemies of Action

1. Fear — It magnifies obstacles and paralyzes decisions.

2. Procrastination — 'Tomorrow' is the excuse that kills vision.

3. Laziness — The lazy man always says, 'There's a lion in the way.'

4. Doubt — Doubt questions what God has already confirmed.

5. Distraction — Divided focus destroys productivity.

A Call to Start Now

Not taking action is like a builder who keeps collecting materials but never starts construction — the materials will eventually rot. Don't let your ideas die in the storage room of hesitation. Today — not tomorrow — is the time to act. Be bold, be diligent, and let your results silence your mockers. "Whatever your hand finds to do, do it with all your might." (Ecclesiastes 9:10)

Interactive Q&A

Q1: What is the difference between an idea and a goal?
A1: An idea is a thought or concept; a goal is a defined and measurable direction that makes the idea specific.

Q2: What is planning, and why is it important?
A2: Planning is creating smaller, actionable steps toward your goal. Without planning, you risk failure and frustration.

Q3: What is 'the king of them all'?
A3: Action — because nothing happens until you act.

Q4: When is the right time to act?
A4: Today — not tomorrow. Delays and procrastination destroy progress.

Q5: What keeps people from taking action?
A5: Fear, laziness, procrastination, self-doubt, and lack of focus.

Reflection Points

- Do I have only ideas, or do I have clear goals?
- Have I written down a practical plan for my goals?
- What fears are holding me back from acting?
- Am I waiting for the perfect time instead of trusting God's timing?
- How can I turn one of my ideas into action today?

Closing Prayer

Heavenly Father, thank You for the power of wisdom and action. Forgive me for the times I have hesitated or feared to move forward. Fill me with clarity to turn ideas into goals, goals into plans, and plans into actions. Strengthen my hands for the work ahead. Let every vision You've placed in my heart come to pass through Your grace. In Jesus' name, Amen.

Chapter 59

Breaking Free from Financial Debt
(Romans 13:8; Proverbs 22:7)

> *"Owe no man any thing, but to love one another: for he that loveth another hath fulfilled the law." (Romans 13:8)*
> *"The rich ruleth over the poor, and the borrower is servant to the lender." (Proverbs 22:7)*

Introduction

Debt is one of the greatest forms of bondage in modern life. Many people today live under the heavy burden of loans, credit cards, and unpaid bills — constantly working, yet never free. The Bible speaks clearly about financial debt, not to condemn us, but to guide us into wisdom and freedom. God wants His children to live as lenders and not borrowers (Deuteronomy 28:12). Debt in itself is not always sinful, but it is dangerous. It limits generosity, steals peace, and often becomes a tool of the enemy to trap believers in anxiety and fear.

Understanding Debt from a Biblical Viewpoint

Debt means owing someone what belongs to them. The Bible never encourages borrowing — it tolerates it under certain conditions, but warns against its consequences. Debt makes you a servant (Proverbs 22:7). When you owe, your freedom is restricted. You must work not just for yourself, but for your creditor. Debt delays destiny and can be a sign of poor stewardship. God entrusts resources to us so we can manage them wisely, just as Jesus emphasized in the parable of the talents (Matthew 25:14–30).

Causes of Financial Debt

1. Lack of Financial Discipline — spending more than you earn.

2. Impulse Buying — purchasing wants instead of needs.

3. Lack of Planning — no budget, no savings, no record-keeping.

4. Covetousness and Comparison — trying to live like others.

5. Poor Giving Habits — withholding offerings closes the door to divine provision (2 Corinthians 9:6).

6. Unbelief and Fear — not trusting that God can provide without borrowing.

7. Greed and Get-Rich-Quick Schemes — impatience leads to traps (Proverbs 28:20).

Debt does not begin in the pocket; it begins in the mindset. Wrong thinking about money leads to wrong living with money.

God's Plan for Financial Freedom

Be a good steward — Recognize that all resources belong to God (Psalm 24:1). Manage money prayerfully.

Live within your means — Avoid unnecessary luxury and learn contentment (1 Timothy 6:8).

Save wisely — Saving is preparation for the future (Proverbs 21:20; Genesis 41:34–36).

Give faithfully — God blesses givers. Tithing opens heaven's windows of provision (Malachi 3:10).

Avoid unnecessary borrowing — If you must borrow, do so with purpose and ability to repay.

4. Steps to Break Free from Debt

1. Acknowledge the Problem — Confession brings freedom (1 John 1:9).

2. Seek God's Mercy and Guidance — Pray for wisdom to reorder your finances.

3. Make a Plan to Pay Back — Write down your debts and set a repayment plan.

4. Cut Down on Expenses — Distinguish between needs and wants.

5. Create Multiple Streams of Income — Use your skills and time wisely (Acts 18:3).

6. Develop a Spirit of Contentment — Stop competing or comparing.

7. Stay Faithful in Giving — Honor God with your substance (Proverbs 3:9–10).

5. The Dangers of Debt

• It steals peace — you live in worry and guilt.

• It kills generosity — you cannot help others when you owe everyone.

• It destroys testimony — a believer who cannot pay his debts loses credibility.

• It limits divine trust — God will not entrust greater resources to one who misuses the little.

Trusting God as Your Source

At the root of all debt is a lack of trust in God's provision. Jesus taught in Matthew 6:33, "Seek ye first the kingdom of God, and his righteousness; and all these things shall be added unto you." When we put God first — in our work, giving, and spending — He takes responsibility for our needs. The secret to financial freedom is not more money; it is more faith and obedience. God is able to supply every need (Philippians 4:19). He will open doors of opportunity when you walk in righteousness and stewardship.

Interactive Q&A

Q1: Is borrowing a sin?
A1: Borrowing is not a sin, but it is not God's best. It brings limitations and can easily lead to bondage.

Q2: How can believers avoid debt?
A2: By planning, saving, living within their means, and trusting God as their provider.

Q3: What is the first step to becoming debt-free?
A3: Acknowledging the problem, repenting of mismanagement, and asking God for wisdom.

Q4: Does tithing help in financial freedom?
A4: Yes. Honouring God with your first fruits opens the door to divine provision and peace (Proverbs 3:9–10).

Q5: What is God's desire for His children financially?
A5: That they prosper, be good stewards, and live as lenders, not borrowers (Deuteronomy 28:12).

Reflection Points

- Am I living within my means or beyond them?
- Do I see money as a tool to serve God or as a master I must serve?
- What practical steps can I take to reduce or eliminate my debts?
- How can I honour God more with my finances?
- Do I trust God enough to believe that He can meet my needs without borrowing?

Closing Prayer

Heavenly Father, thank You for being my Provider. I confess that I have sometimes managed money unwisely and allowed debt to control my life. Please forgive me. Give me wisdom to manage resources faithfully and discipline to live within my means. I receive grace to break free from every financial bondage. Let Your blessing make me rich and add no sorrow to it (Proverbs 10:22). I declare that I am a lender and not a borrower. In Jesus' mighty name, Amen.

Chapter 60

Marriage: As Ordained by God

(Genesis 2:18–24; Matthew 19:4–6; Ephesians 5:31–33)

"And the LORD God said, It is not good that the man should be alone; I will make him an help meet for him."
(Genesis 2:18)
"Therefore shall a man leave his father and his mother, and shall cleave unto his wife: and they shall be one flesh."
(Genesis 2:24)

Introduction

Marriage is not a human invention — it is a divine institution, ordained by God from the very beginning. Before there was a nation, a government, or even a church, there was marriage. It was designed by God for companionship, love, fruitfulness, and the reflection of His own covenant relationship with His people.

In a world where marriage is often misunderstood, redefined, or neglected, believers must return to the biblical foundation: **marriage is sacred, permanent, and purposeful.** It is a covenant before God, not a casual contract between two people.

The Origin of Marriage

Marriage was first instituted in the Garden of Eden. God saw Adam's loneliness and declared, *"It is not good that the man should be alone"* (Genesis 2:18). Eve was created not as an afterthought but as a perfect companion — equal in value, distinct in role, and united in purpose.

The joining of Adam and Eve marks the first wedding ceremony, with God Himself as the officiator. He brought the woman to the man (Genesis 2:22), blessing their union and establishing the pattern for all generations.

Marriage, therefore, is not man's idea — it is **God's idea**. It is holy, honourable, and designed to be a lifelong covenant.

The Purpose of Marriage

The Bible reveals several divine purposes for marriage:

1. **Companionship** — God created marriage to meet the human need for fellowship and intimacy (Genesis 2:18).

2. **Partnership** — The man and woman are called to work together as a team in life and in faith (Ecclesiastes 4:9–12).

3. **Procreation** — Through marriage, God's command to "be fruitful and multiply" (Genesis 1:28) is fulfilled.

4. **Purity** — Marriage provides a holy environment for physical intimacy and helps believers avoid immorality (1 Corinthians 7:2).

5. **Reflection of Christ and the Church** — In Ephesians 5:31–32, Paul explains that marriage is a symbol of the relationship between Christ (the Bridegroom) and His Church (the Bride).

Marriage is not just for happiness — it is for holiness. It is God's tool to shape our character, teach us sacrificial love, and model the Gospel to the world.

God's Design for Marriage

In Matthew 19:4–6, Jesus reaffirmed God's design for marriage:

"Have ye not read, that he which made them at the beginning made them male and female… For this cause shall a man leave father and mother, and shall cleave to his wife: and they twain shall be one flesh?"

From this, we learn four key truths:

1. **Marriage is between a man and a woman** — not two men, two women, or any other combination.

2. **Marriage is exclusive** — one man, one woman, united under God.

3. **Marriage is permanent** — "What God hath joined together, let not man put asunder" (Matthew 19:6).

4. **Marriage is sacred** — God Himself joins the couple and witnesses their covenant (Malachi 2:14–15).

Any attempt to redefine marriage apart from these divine principles leads to confusion, pain, and disorder in society.

The Responsibilities within Marriage

Marriage flourishes when both husband and wife understand and honour their God-given roles.

For the Husband:

- Love your wife sacrificially, as Christ loved the Church (Ephesians 5:25).
- Lead your family with humility, wisdom, and integrity.
- Provide for your home and protect it spiritually and physically (1 Timothy 5:8).

For the Wife:

- Submit to your husband as unto the Lord (Ephesians 5:22).
- Support and respect your husband's leadership.
- Build your home with love, prayer, and wisdom (Proverbs 14:1; Titus 2:4–5).

Both are called to mutual respect, understanding, and forgiveness. A successful marriage is not built on competition but on **cooperation** — two people working together under the leadership of God.

The Covenant of Marriage

Marriage is not a contract that can be broken when feelings fade — it is a covenant sealed before God. In Malachi 2:14, God calls the husband and wife *"companions"* bound by a covenant.

A covenant is based on commitment, not convenience. It endures through seasons of joy and trial, prosperity and hardship. Love is not just a feeling — it is a decision to remain faithful, forgiving, and devoted.

When God is the third cord in the union (Ecclesiastes 4:12), that marriage cannot easily be broken.

Challenges and the Grace to Overcome

Every marriage faces storms — misunderstandings, financial pressures, spiritual warfare, or emotional struggles. Yet, God provides grace to overcome them.

Pray together.
Forgive quickly.
Communicate openly.
Keep Christ at the center.

A marriage that kneels together will always stand together.

The Reward of a Godly Marriage

When a couple honours God in their marriage:

1. Their home becomes a sanctuary of peace.
2. Their children are blessed and secure.
3. Their union becomes a testimony to others.

Psalm 128:1–3 beautifully describes this:

"Blessed is every one that feareth the LORD; that walketh in his ways... Thy wife shall be as a fruitful vine by the sides of thine house: thy children like olive plants round about thy table."

Interactive Q&A

Q1: Who instituted marriage, and why is that important?
A1: God Himself instituted marriage (Genesis 2:18–24). It reminds us that marriage is sacred and should follow His divine pattern.

Q2: What are the main purposes of marriage?
A2: Companionship, partnership, procreation, purity, and reflection of Christ and the Church.

Q3: What is the difference between a covenant and a contract in marriage?
A3: A contract is based on mutual benefit; a covenant is based on unconditional commitment before God.

Q4: How can couples overcome challenges in marriage?
A4: Through prayer, forgiveness, communication, humility, and dependence on God's Word.

Q5: What is the greatest key to a lasting marriage?
A5: Making Christ the foundation and center of the relationship.

Reflection Points

- Is God truly the center of my marriage (or future marriage)?
- Do I see marriage as a covenant or as a contract?
- How do I demonstrate love, respect, and forgiveness in my relationship?
-What steps can I take to strengthen my home and reflect Christ through it?

Closing Prayer

Heavenly Father, thank You for the gift of marriage. You designed it to be holy, joyful, and fruitful. Lord, help us to build our marriages on Your Word and to love each other with the love of Christ. Heal broken homes, strengthen weak ones, and bless every union that honours Your name. May our marriages reflect Your covenant love to the world. In Jesus' name, Amen.

Chapter 61

Spiritual Growth and Maturity

(Ephesians 4:13–15; Hebrews 5:12–14; 2 Peter 3:18)

"Till we all come in the unity of the faith, and of the knowledge of the Son of God, unto a perfect man, unto the measure of the stature of the fulness of Christ."
(Ephesians 4:13)

"For when for the time ye ought to be teachers, ye have need that one teach you again which be the first principles of the oracles of God; and are become such as have need of milk, and not of strong meat... But strong meat belongeth to them that are of full age..." (Hebrews 5:12–14)

"But grow in grace, and in the knowledge of our Lord and Saviour Jesus Christ." (2 Peter 3:18)

Introduction

Every child of God is born again through faith in Jesus Christ, but not every believer grows into maturity. Salvation is a birth; spiritual maturity is a journey. Just as a newborn baby must be nurtured to grow into strength and wisdom, so every believer must develop spiritually to fulfil God's purpose. God's desire is not just to save us, but to shape us into the image of His Son.

Spiritual growth means moving from immaturity to maturity, from milk to meat, from instability to stability. The Christian life is not a stagnant experience — it is a continuous journey of transformation through the Word of God and the power of the Holy Spirit.

Understanding Spiritual Growth

Spiritual growth is the process of becoming more like Christ in character, conduct, and conviction. It is the inward transformation that results in outward holiness. True spiritual growth produces humility, love, and obedience to God's Word.

To grow spiritually means:
- To be increasingly conformed to the image of Christ (Romans 8:29).
- To increase in the knowledge and application of God's Word.
- To produce the fruit of the Spirit (Galatians 5:22–23).

- To move from dependence on others to personal maturity and discernment.

The Stages of Spiritual Growth

The Bible uses physical development to describe spiritual growth:
1. Newborn believers — needing milk (1 Peter 2:2).
2. Young believers — strong and overcoming temptation (1 John 2:14).
3. Mature believers — discerning good and evil, walking in wisdom (Hebrews 5:14).

The Warning Against Immaturity

In Hebrews 5:12–14, believers are rebuked for remaining spiritual infants when they should have been teachers. Spiritual immaturity keeps many from fulfilling their potential. Milk represents the elementary principles of faith, while strong meat represents deeper understanding and maturity. God wants His people to move beyond the basics and grow in righteousness and discernment.

Why Spiritual Growth Matters

1. It pleases God — Growth reflects obedience and fruitfulness.
2. It equips believers — Mature Christians are stable and discerning.
3. It glorifies Christ — Our growth reflects His nature.
4. It prepares us for service — God entrusts responsibilities to the mature.

Hindrances to Spiritual Growth

- Neglect of Scripture and prayer.
- Unconfessed sin and disobedience.
- Pride and unwillingness to learn.
- Distractions from worldly pleasures.
- Lack of fellowship and accountability.

Steps to Spiritual Growth

1. Feed daily on the Word of God (Joshua 1:8).
2. Develop a consistent prayer life.
3. Walk in obedience to God's Word (James 1:22).
4. Fellowship with other believers (Hebrews 10:25).
5. Serve in God's kingdom (Matthew 20:26–28).
6. Endure trials with faith (James 1:2–4).
7. Depend daily on the Holy Spirit (Galatians 5:16).

The Measure of True Maturity

True maturity is reflected not in knowledge alone, but in character. It is seen in love, humility, faithfulness, and discernment. A mature believer is stable, self-controlled, forgiving, and Christlike in attitude.

Pressing On Toward Perfection

Spiritual maturity is a lifelong pursuit. Paul said, 'Not as though I had already attained... but I press toward the mark' (Philippians 3:12–14). Keep pressing forward — growing in prayer, love, wisdom, and the Word. God's goal is that Christ be formed in us completely.

Interactive Q&A

Q1: What does spiritual growth mean?
A1: Becoming more like Christ through the renewing of the mind, obedience to the Word, and the Spirit's power.

Q2: Why is spiritual maturity important?
A2: It prepares us for greater service and helps us stand firm in trials.

Q3: What causes spiritual stagnation?
A3: Neglect of prayer and the Word, sin, and worldliness.

Q4: What are signs of maturity?
A4: Love, humility, obedience, and discernment.

Q5: How can believers grow into maturity?
A5: Through study, prayer, obedience, fellowship, and walking in the Spirit.

Reflection Points

- Am I growing or stagnating in my faith?
- What habits are hindering my growth?
- Do I help others grow spiritually?
- How can I move from milk to strong meat in my spiritual life?

Closing Prayer

Heavenly Father, thank You for saving me and giving me new life in Christ. Help me to grow in grace, faith, and understanding. Teach me to move from spiritual infancy to maturity, to reflect Christ in all I do. Strengthen me through Your Spirit and keep me steadfast until I reach the fullness of Christ. In Jesus' name, Amen.

Chapter 62

The Gifts of the Spirit

(1 Corinthians 12:1–11; Romans 12:6–8; Ephesians 4:11–13)

"Now concerning spiritual gifts, brethren, I would not have you ignorant... But the manifestation of the Spirit is given to every man to profit withal." (1 Corinthians 12:1, 7)

Introduction

The gifts of the Spirit are divine abilities given by the Holy Spirit to believers for the building up of the Church and the advancement of God's kingdom. They are not earned by merit or effort — they are gifts of grace, given according to God's will and purpose. When a believer receives the Holy

Spirit, they not only receive power for holy living but also spiritual enablement for service. The gifts are evidence of God's active presence among His people, revealing Christ to the world.

The Apostle Paul addressed the Corinthian church — a congregation rich in gifts but divided by pride — to remind them that spiritual gifts are meant for unity, service, and edification, not competition or self-glory.

Understanding Spiritual Gifts

The Greek word for 'gifts' in 1 Corinthians 12 is 'charismata,' meaning 'grace gifts.' These are supernatural empowerments that go beyond natural human ability. Spiritual gifts differ from natural talents because they operate under divine anointing. For instance, someone with the gift of teaching not only communicates truth but also imparts revelation that transforms lives.

Paul teaches that 'there are diversities of gifts, but the same Spirit' (1 Corinthians 12:4). The Holy Spirit is the source of all gifts, distributing them as He wills (1 Corinthians 12:11).

The Purpose of Spiritual Gifts

Spiritual gifts are not for personal gain or display, but for the common good — 'to profit withal.' Their purpose includes:

- To glorify Jesus Christ (John 16:14)
- To build and strengthen the Church (Ephesians 4:12)
- To serve others with love (1 Peter 4:10)
- To confirm the Word with signs (Mark 16:20)
- To reveal the Holy Spirit's power (1 Corinthians 2:4)

The Nine Gifts of the Spirit (1 Corinthians 12:8–10)

Paul lists nine distinct gifts which can be grouped into three categories:

A. The Gifts of Revelation (To Know the Mind of God)

1. Word of Wisdom — Divine insight into God's purpose and guidance in complex situations.
2. Word of Knowledge — Supernatural revelation of facts unknown by human means.
3. Discerning of Spirits — The ability to recognize whether a spirit is from God, man, or the enemy.

B. The Gifts of Power (To Demonstrate the Power of God)

4. Gift of Faith — Supernatural confidence to believe God for the impossible.

5. Gifts of Healing — Divine ability to bring physical, emotional, or spiritual restoration.
6. Working of Miracles — God's supernatural intervention that defies natural law.

C. The Gifts of Inspiration (To Speak by the Spirit of God)

7. Prophecy — Speaking the heart and mind of God for edification, exhortation, and comfort.
8. Divers Kinds of Tongues — Speaking languages unknown to the speaker but inspired by God.
9. Interpretation of Tongues — Understanding and communicating the message spoken in tongues.

The Unity in Diversity of Gifts

Though there are many gifts, the Spirit is one. Just as the human body has many members that work together, so does the Body of Christ. Every believer has a role. No gift is superior to another — all are necessary for the Church to function effectively (1 Corinthians 12:12–27).

The Right Attitude Toward Spiritual Gifts

1. Humility — Every gift is by grace, not merit (Romans 12:3).
2. Love — Without love, gifts lose their value (1 Corinthians

13:1–3).
3. Submission — Gifts must operate under divine order and authority.
4. Service — Gifts exist to serve others, not to elevate self (1 Peter 4:10).
5. Discernment — Use gifts with wisdom, ensuring they align with Scripture.

The Fruit and the Gifts

Spiritual gifts demonstrate the power of the Spirit, while the fruit of the Spirit reveals the character of Christ (Galatians 5:22–23). Having gifts without fruit leads to imbalance. Gifts attract people, but character keeps them. The mature believer pursues both power and purity.

How to Receive and Operate in the Gifts of the Spirit

1. Desire earnestly — 'Covet earnestly the best gifts' (1 Corinthians 12:31).
2. Pray and ask — God gives His Spirit to those who ask (Luke 11:13).
3. Be filled with the Spirit (Ephesians 5:18).
4. Walk in obedience — disobedience quenches the Spirit (1 Thessalonians 5:19).
5. Use your gift faithfully (2 Timothy 1:6).
6. Stay humble — give glory to God, not to self.

The Balance Between Gifts and Order

Paul instructed the Corinthians that spiritual gifts must operate with wisdom and order: 'Let all things be done decently and in order' (1 Corinthians 14:40). The Holy Spirit is not the author of confusion but of peace (1 Corinthians 14:33). A Spirit-filled church is both powerful and disciplined.

Interactive Q&A

Q1: What is the purpose of the gifts of the Spirit?
A1: To build up the Church, glorify God, and serve others.

Q2: Are spiritual gifts only for leaders?
A2: No, every believer has at least one gift from the Holy Spirit (1 Corinthians 12:7).

Q3: How can I discover my spiritual gifts?
A3: Through prayer, service, and guidance from the Holy Spirit and mature believers.

Q4: Can gifts operate without love?
A4: Yes, but they lose their eternal value (1 Corinthians 13:1–3).

Q5: How can gifts be used responsibly?

A5: By operating in humility, under authority, and according to God's Word.

Reflection Points

- Do I know which spiritual gifts God has given me?
- Am I using my gifts to serve others or to seek recognition?
- Do I exercise my gifts in love and humility?
- How can I balance the fruit and gifts of the Spirit in my life?

Closing Prayer

Heavenly Father, thank You for the gifts of the Holy Spirit. Fill me with Your presence and empower me to use these gifts to glorify Your name and serve others. Help me to walk in love, humility, and obedience as I operate under Your divine guidance. Let my life be a vessel through which Your Spirit moves to heal, save, and transform lives. In Jesus' name, Amen.

About the Author

Pastor Hartley Edorodion is the senior pastor of Complete Christianity and Holy Ghost Power Ministry, headquartered in Newcastle, England. With a heart for teaching and a passion for making scripture accessible, Pastor Edorodion has authored numerous inspirational works aimed at helping believers grow in faith and understanding.

In "Bible Walk," he invites readers on a flexible journey through the scriptures, suitable for personal devotion, small groups, and study gatherings alike. Outside of writing and ministry, Pastor Edorodion shares insights and updates on his social media platforms, connecting with a global community of faith.

You can connect with him and follow his teachings online:

- Email: edorodion@hotmail.com
- Facebook: facebook.com/hartley.edorodion
- Instagram: instagram.com/hartleyedorodion
- TikTok: tiktok.com/@hartleyedorodion
- X (Twitter): x.com/HEdorodion
- YouTube: youtube.com/@hartleyedorodion

www.ingramcontent.com/pod-product-compliance
Lightning Source LLC
Chambersburg PA
CBHW020322170426
43200CB00006B/236